*Five*
# Mennonites
## and a Greek

# *Five* Mennonites and a Greek

Ilona Abrahams *with*

Dora Goerzen

Darlene Schroeder

Sharon Unruh

Lois Voth

Lynne Voth

| Copyright: | ©2016 Ilona Abrahams |
| Text: | ©2016 Ilona Abrahams |
| Photography: | ©2016 Ilona Abrahams |
| | ©2016 Fern Bartel, |
| | cover photo and pages 13, 28, 31, 36, 45, 49, |
| | 51, 55, 56, 69, 90 |

Five Mennonites and a Greek/Ilona Abrahams, 2016

Library of Congress Control Number: 2016935250
ISBN: 978-0-9968689-0-7

Printed in the United States of America
Printed by: Mennonite Press Inc.

| Design and Layout: | Nancy Miller |
| Written by: | Ilona Abrahams |
| Edited by: | Marjorie Shoemaker |
| Published by: | ISA Pages |

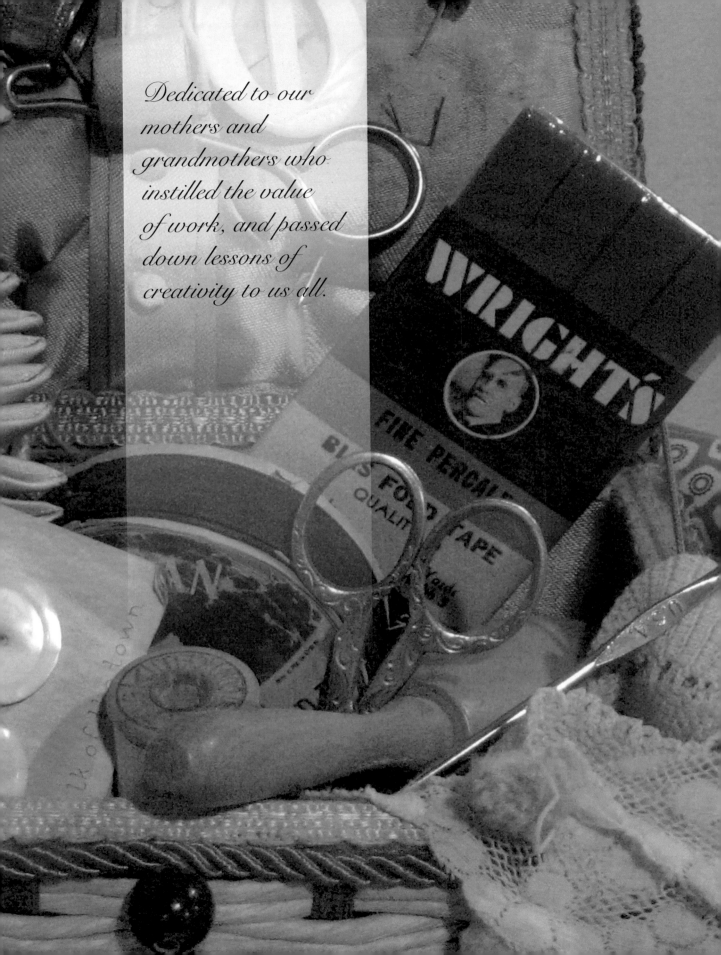

*Dedicated to our mothers and grandmothers who instilled the value of work, and passed down lessons of creativity to us all.*

# Table of contents

*Preface*

# The button jar

Grandmother slowly wiped her hands on her apron. While her granddaughter waited with anticipation, she opened the cupboard door and reached inside. Carefully she picked up the jar and placed it on the table. As she unscrewed the lid and tipped the jar, the buttons poured out, a kaleidoscope of colors, endless sizes and shapes scattering across the tabletop. Gently touching the buttons, Grandmother began to tell their stories. Memories came flooding back as she selected the dull, gray buttons that came from her husband's old work shirts. She closed her fingers around the pearly white buttons she had clipped from her wedding dress and used on her daughter's baptism dress. The five large emerald buttons strung together on a safety pin had once graced the beautiful coat she received as an engagement present from her future husband. The button jar held a mere collection of buttons, a lifetime of memories, and stories a granddaughter waited to hear.

In a time when nothing was wasted, every homemaker had a button jar or another place where discarded buttons were kept. She removed the buttons from articles of clothing as the garments wore out. Some buttons were tied together with string while others were simply tossed into the jar. Whether she was looking for a sturdy button to mend a work shirt or for the perfect button to complete a dress for her daughter's doll, there were always buttons waiting to be reused.

In many ways, we are like those buttons in the button jar. We also come in a variety of sizes, shapes, and color. No two of us are alike, nor would we want to be. We are all tossed together and expected to get along. Each of us is given a role to play. What are your stories? What makes you unique?

*Five Mennonites and a Greek* is our story. We are like the buttons in the button jar. In many ways, we are very different. We originate from an assortment of backgrounds and have a plethora of interests. We come from three states, two countries, and three religious traditions, but remarkably, we now all attend the same church. Somehow, we have been strung together on a string, supporting each other, laughing together, and in the process, creating a lifetime of memories.

## *Five Mennonites and a Greek –* The Connection

One evening at a monthly meeting I jokingly made the comment that if we were to write a book about our group; we could call it Five Mennonites and a Greek. At the time, we all laughed. Occasionally we would talk about it but it wasn't until the summer of 2014 that I decided to get a bit more serious. After some discerning, the group decided to give more thought to the idea.

The six of us started meeting in 2010. Earlier we had all been part of a group that had disbanded. Later a number of people began to think about forming a new group that would focus on our hobbies; what we did after work, after supper was cooked, after the dishes were done. That small amount of time we try to squeeze out of a routine day.

People began to think about the options available, and after a period of time six of us decided to meet monthly. At the time we were all employed outside the home. But the thought of meeting one evening a month to work on projects, share, ask questions, find answers, or just listen to each other became a time we all looked forward to and our group began. A pot of fresh coffee, iced tea, and some delicious dessert always completes the feeling of hospitality we experience when coming to each other's homes.

So why name the book Five Mennonites and a Greek? All six of us live within a ten-mile radius of each other, and all attend Tabor Mennonite Church. Interestingly enough, none of us attended the same church while growing up.

Darlene Schroeder grew up in the Goessel community and attended Goessel schools. Darlene came from a General Conference Mennonite farm family and grew up attending Tabor Mennonite Church.

Ilona Abrahams grew up on a farm northeast of Goessel, Kansas and went to Alexanderwohl Mennonite Church, where most of her ancestors had attended. Upon marrying, she began attending Tabor Church.

Sharon Unruh was raised on a farm near Hillsboro, Kansas, a town about 16 miles northeast of Goessel. She grew up attending the Mennonite Brethren Church in Hillsboro. She eventually found her way to the Goessel community when she married. She and her husband began attending Tabor Church, after moving to the family homestead.

Lois Voth spent the first twenty-four years of her life on a farm near Corn, Oklahoma. She attended Corn Mennonite Brethren Church. In time, she moved to Hillsboro, Kansas, met her husband, moved to the family farm southeast of Goessel, and began attending Tabor Church.

Lynne Voth spent her childhood on a farm near Freeman, South Dakota where she attended Salem Zion Mennonite Church. While living in Kansas for a year of voluntary service, she met her husband, and they settled on the family farm southeast of Goessel. Her husband had grown up in Tabor Church, so they continued to attend there.

Dora Goerzen grew up on the island of Crete in Greece and participated in the Greek Eastern Orthodox Church. Through relatives, she met her future husband, who was in Greece with the Mennonite Central Committee Pax program. They were soon married, and after some time made the decision to move back to Kansas and raise their family in the Goessel community. As it was, her husband had been raised in and attended Tabor Church.

All of us come from various Mennonite backgrounds except Dora. She has brought the diversity to the group that is needed. Through her we have learned about an entirely different culture and have been the recipients of many delightful ethnic Greek foods. She has attempted to teach us how to cook some of them and in turn has learned more about the history of Mennonite food. Recipes from both Greek and Mennonite cultures are shared in this book.

Occasionally we take field trips. We chose a number of our favorite field trips and share them with you in the following pages.

We all enjoy quilting in some form and have visited various fabric stores individually or as a group. In this book we address why we appreciate the art of quilting and share some of the quilts each of us has made.

Sharing our faith is an important aspect of our lives. Whether we do this in our jobs, in conversations with the people we meet while we shop, or through a broader entity such as the Kansas Mennonite Relief Sale, we look for ways to serve others.

We still continue to meet once a month. Now, all but one of us has retired. Schedules are not so rigid, and evening meetings can stretch a bit longer as we linger over another cup of coffee. More time can be given to the projects our hands itch to create.

Chapter 3 of Ecclesiastes, states there is a time for everything, a time to weep, and a time to laugh. Each year brings joys and challenges. Children get married, and grandchildren are born. Parents pass on, and illnesses creep in when least expected. And mixed in throughout these seasons of life, we find fulfillment in what we do. This is a true gift from God.

*there is a time for everything, a time to weep, and a time to laugh*

# OUR HANDS

*"Whatever your hand finds to do, do it with all your might…"* —*Ecclesiastes 9:10a (NIV)*

Look at your hands. What do they tell you about your life? Are they smooth and supple? Perhaps they are the hands of a young mother prepared to soothe a small child. Possibly they are beginning to show some age, hands that have cared for and raised a family. Maybe your hands are wrinkled and bent, proclaiming a full life. As we study our hands, we begin to realize they are a roadmap of our life. They comprise a wealth of wisdom and commemorate a lifetime of love.

Our hands are a tool God has given us to reach out and embrace life. Each day the scars and marks accumulate and show how we have used these tools to accomplish God's work. What we do with our hands has a significant impact on those we come in contact with every day.

If you have reached out and shaken the hand of a homeless person, your hands showed compassion and brought a little ray of hope into someone's life. Your hands have blessed someone with hospitality when you created a delicious meal and welcomed them to the community, neighborhood or church family. Perhaps your hands worked alongside, someone whose home had been destroyed by a tornado. As you took another's hand in yours and prayed with them, you may have given them strength to deal with an unforeseen tragedy.

Whether we recognize it or not, God continually encourages us to extend our hands to others and share his gift of life.

In Proverbs 139:9-10, God promises that HIS hand will lead us and hold us fast. Someday our hands will reach out to God, as he calls us home. Then our hands will rest, and we will be securely embraced in the hands of God.

*I am a teacher. In order to be a good teacher you have to love children unconditionally.*

*I have always loved children, but I haven't always been a teacher. In the fall of 1990, I felt God leading me to finish my Elementary Education degree. Eventually, with the encouragement of family members and friends, I returned to college and earned my elementary degree. God knew all along what my gifts are. He was just patiently waiting for me to figure it out.*

*Every day when I walk into my classroom, look at my students and see the sparkle in their eyes, I realize that God has truly blessed me. While using my hands, I am able to help mold some of his most precious creations.*
—Ilona Abrahams

*Goessel Elementary School cooks are known for their delicious lunches. All meals are prepared at the school. Breads and cookies are made from scratch. Students and staff eagerly anticipate lunch when the aroma of fresh baked bread begins to drift down the halls. Occasionally, we are treated with cookies, such as these Angel cookies.*

# ANGEL COOKIES

INGREDIENTS:

$3\frac{1}{2}$ lbs. of oleo
$3\frac{1}{2}$ cups of brown sugar
$3\frac{1}{2}$ cups of white sugar
8 eggs
16 cups of flour

8 teaspoons soda
1 teaspoon salt
1 teaspoon cream of tarter
3 tablespoons vanilla

DIRECTIONS:

Preheat oven to 350° F. Lightly grease cookie sheet. In a large bowl, cream the oleo and sugars. Add the eggs and vanilla; mix well. Stir in the flour, soda, salt, and cream of tarter until well combined. Using a #40 ice-cream dipper, drop level dipperfulls onto prepared cookie sheet. Bake 14-15 minutes. Cool on wire rack and remove from pan.

Makes 20 dozen

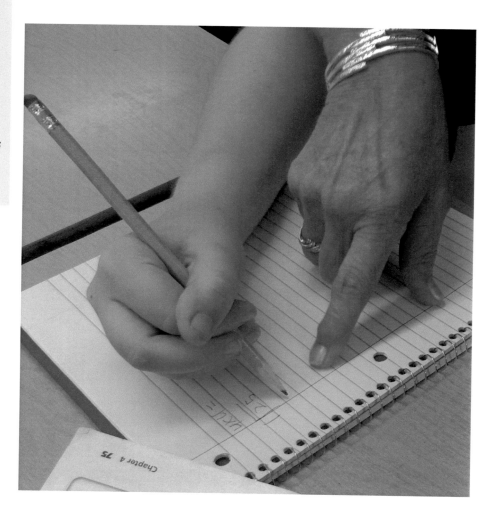

# APRICOT JAM

INGREDIENTS:
3 pounds fully ripe apricots
1/3 cup water
3 cups sugar

2 tablespoons lemon juice
1 tablespoon butter

DIRECTIONS:
Wash and pit apricots. Chop the fruit and measure 4½ cups. In a large kettle or Dutch oven, combine apricots and water. Bring to boil. Cover and simmer 5-10 minutes, or until apricots are tender. Stir frequently. Add the sugar and lemon juice; mix well. Stir until sugar dissolves. Add one tablespoon butter to prevent the mixture from foaming.

Bring to a full rolling boil. Cook 7- 8 minutes, constantly stirring until desired thickness is reached. Remove from heat and skim off foam. Pour at once into hot sterilized jars and seal, or pour into jars, cool and freeze.

Makes 5½ pints

As I grew up, gardening was a part of my summer experience. Each spring my mother planted a huge garden to provide produce for the coming summer and winter. Weeding and hoeing were tedious tasks, and everything was done by hand.

After I married I planted my own garden. Now, I look forward to receiving gardening catalogs in winter and placing my order. When spring finally arrives, it is a joy to sow the small seeds and wait for them to sprout.

The results of all our efforts are the produce we gather from the garden. It is satisfying to pick and prepare the vegetables I have grown.

Nature and gardening are therapeutic and calming. It feels good to be outdoors after a long, cold winter.

I also enjoy planting and tending to a variety of flowers. Potting new plants and transplanting old ones brings a sense of satisfaction.

As I work outside and the soil sifts through my hands, I am reminded of the beauty of God's world.
—Lynne Voth

Quilting has been a part of my family life from the time I was born. My first quilting experience was when I was in 5th or 6th grade. That summer I couldn't go to Vacation Bible School because I had come down with the mumps. While the others were in school, my mom and I would go to Grandma's house. Grandma happened to have a quilt in the frame and allowed me to help her quilt. I was surprised when Grandma gave me the quilt when it was finished.

Quilting has become an activity my whole family enjoys. In 1999 my sisters and sisters-in-law decided to make a quilt for each of the nineteen grandchildren as a wedding gift. So far, we have made thirteen different and distinctive quilts.

Using our hands to cut, piece, and quilt brings our family together while creating wonderful memories in the process.
—Lois Voth

We usually spend a weekend together when we make quilts for family members. Several people are in charge of making a meal. We keep meal preparation at a minimum by fixing soups or casseroles. Sometimes the children help with the preparation so the adults can keep working.

# CHICKEN NOODLE DANDY

INGREDIENTS:

2 cans cream of chicken soup
¾ cup sour cream
1 teaspoon salt
¼ teaspoon each pepper and ground sage

4 cups cooked noodles
3 cups cubed chicken
2 cups cooked peas

DIRECTIONS:

In a large saucepan, blend soup and sour cream. Add remaining ingredients. Heat while stirring occasionally.
Pour into 2 – 1½ quart casserole dishes.
Bake at 350° for 30-40 minutes or until bubbly.

This dish freezes well. When thawed, stir in ¼ cup water and reheat. Place in a cold oven. Bake at 400° for 1 hour and 15 minutes. Stir before serving. Variation: Can also be made with your choice of soup, vegetables, and spices.

Makes 10 cups

# MOM'S CUTOUT COOKIES

INGREDIENTS:

½ cup butter
1 cup sugar
3 cups flour

½ teaspoon vanilla
2 eggs
½ teaspoon soda

DIRECTIONS:

Cream butter and sugar together until light.
Add eggs one at a time, beating well after each addition. Add the vanilla.
Sift flour and soda together and add to creamed mixture so the dough holds together. Chill.

Roll the dough on a lightly floured surface to the desired thickness and cut with your favorite cookie cutter.

Bake at 365° for 7-10 minutes. Bottom should be lightly browned. Do not overbake.

Frost with your favorite frosting.

Note: I always double the recipe.

The thought of being a grandmother sent chills up and down my spine as our second son and his wife began the adoption process of three little girls. Eventually we were blessed with six more grandchildren.

Watching them develop their own personalities and looking for family resemblances is priceless.

Each stage of their lives brings a different set of experiences. What fun when we swim together, and they use their hands to teach me a new technique. I experience so much enjoyment when I help them use their hands to create cookies and decorate them.

One of my biggest joys has been using my hands to teach two of my granddaughters to sew. Watching them use their hands to maneuver the fabric and then seeing the smile on their faces when the project begins to take shape is priceless.

I enjoy watching each one of my grandchildren attempt different activities, whether they are catching a ball, riding a four-wheeler, reading, playing games, or praying. As I use my hands to interact with my nine beautiful grandchildren, I am reminded of how God has blessed me.

—Sharon Unruh

When I was a young girl and had my first piano lesson, I had no idea how important playing piano would be in my life. While my thumbs played middle C and I sang the song, "I am Mr. Middle C, take a good long look at me," the enjoyment of music started growing. Even though the parlor where our upright former player piano was located was cold in winter, I practiced.

I have had four different teachers during my life. Each one has helped me enjoy the time I spend playing piano. I even took lessons from one of the teachers after I was married and had children. I also gave piano lessons to community children.

In church I have played for congregational singing, junior choir, and ladies trio, and at various other times and places.

One of the New Year's resolutions I made this year was to play each song in our church hymnal. I want to keep my fingers limber, so I try to play about 15 minutes a day.

Music is soothing. On Sunday afternoons when I played a variety of songs, my husband enjoyed listening to them

# AUNT FRIEDA'S CHOCOLATE PIE

INGREDIENTS:
4 tablespoons corn starch
2 tablespoons cocoa
1 cup sugar
2 cups water
1 tablespoon butter
1 teaspoon vanilla

DIRECTIONS:
Mix and stir the first four ingredients on the stove until the mixture comes to a boil. Boil one minute and then add the butter and vanilla. Pour into a baked pie crust and let it cool. Top with whipped cream.

while he rested in his recliner. Since he passed away, I play to sooth my grief and comfort myself.

The piano from my childhood has been replaced with a new piano, but the keys are the same and the possibility of using my hands to create music is available anytime.
—Darlene Schroeder

On the farm some animals were pets and others were used for food. In fall my parents would butcher a pig. Relatives would gather and mountains of food would be prepared. I remember coming home from grade school and usually finding a leftover piece of chocolate pie. Interestingly enough the original penciled recipe uses water rather than milk.

# SPANAKOPITA

INGREDIENTS:

1½ pounds of fresh spinach
1 egg, slightly, beaten
1-1pound package Fillo dough
¾ cup olive oil
1 cup Greek feta cheese, crumbled
½ teaspoon dill weed
½ teaspoon salt
¼ teaspoon pepper
6 green onions, chopped

DIRECTIONS:

Filling:

1. Wash spinach, chop into small pieces and place in a colander.
2. Sprinkle ½ teaspoon salt on the spinach and let this stand for 5-10 minutes.
3. Squeeze out excess water and place spinach in a bowl.
4. Add the rest of the ingredients, except save ½ cup oil for later, and mix together.

MAKING THE SPANAKOPITA:

Put two sheets of Fillo dough on a cutting board. Brush each Fillo sheets with oil. Add two more pieces of Fillo and brush with oil. Do this a total of 3 times.

Spread filling thinly over ½ of the dough. Roll up like a jelly roll and place cut side down on a baking sheet. Brush with oil.

With a sharp knife make 1/8 inch deep diagonal cuts into the Fillo roll about 1 inch apart. (Be sure not to cut all the way through into the filling). Bake in a preheated 350° oven for 30-35 minutes. Cool and cut completely. Note: Dough dries out quickly. Keep it covered with a sheet of wax paper and a lightly dampened towel over the wax paper.

*Cooking takes time, practice and patience. I learned to cook out of necessity. My mother died when I was nearly twelve. This left my father, three older brothers and me to take care of the home.*

*Cooking in Greece during the time I was growing up was very time-consuming. Each neighborhood had a fresh fruit and vegetable market and a bakery. There were no canned foods or prepared food; everything was made from scratch.*

*We visited the market every day. Olive oil was bought in large quantities once a year and used in everything. We seldom ate beef. It was too expensive. When we did eat meat, it was usually lamb, goat, or chicken. We purchased squid, octopus, fish, and clams at the fish market. Although fruit was considered our dessert, we always had cookies and sweet breads for the holidays.*

*My father was a gourmet cook. He often cooked time-consuming meals such as stuffed grape leaves.*

*Eventually, I learned to cook because he would begin to make a dish and then tell me to finish it. There were many times the dishes didn't turn out perfect, but my father was a gracious man and with his help, I became successful. Now I take joy in using my hands to recreate some of those same dishes for my family.*

—Dora Goerzen

Pattern: Nottingham Village, Charlotte O'Leary of Quilting Hens Studio
Quilt Maker: Ilona Abrahams

# OUR HANDS CONNECT

*"But if we walk in the light, as he is in the
light, we have fellowship with one another..."*
— I John 1:7 (ESV)

Most of us spend time traveling to destinations we don't often visit. Children and teachers look forward to field trips. These trips provide opportunities for children to experience learning outside the classroom. They allow children to interact with each other and relate to other individuals while offering a more informal learning experience.

God also wants us to experience life. He wants us to take "field trips" and move beyond the four walls of the church. Jesus and his disciples went many places. As they traveled together, they not only learned to know each other better, but also met a variety of people. It was through meeting these people that they began to understand their culture and how to minister to them more effectively.

Many Christians expect to develop spiritually, yet are reluctant to move beyond the church. Although it is important to spend time together when worshiping, we are transformed when we are willing to expose ourselves to what lies beyond. God encourages us to live a life filled with importance, one that has relevance. An existence that is filled with significance connects us to the people outside the church. When we are willing to move outside the church, we can begin to understand others, and pass along God's incredible love.

At some point, we decided we would enjoy taking some field trips. Through these tours, we have met some wonderful people. These people willingly received us into their establishments and readily shared information about their community. Our hope is that we also left something of significance with them.

# Prairie Flower Crafts

All of us enjoy quilts, quilting, piecing, and fabric. So we have been to a number of remarkable stores, where bolts of fabric call your name and beg to be bought. When we first visited Prairie Flower Crafts in Alden, Kansas, we were simply overwhelmed. Rooms of fabric displayed every color, type and texture imaginable.

In May 1970, Sara Sleeper bought the Alden Mercantile Store. She immediately began transforming the store. One-half became Alden Village Grocery, and the other half became a small fabric shop, Prairie Flower Crafts.

In the beginning, Sara stocked the store with 100% cotton fabric, calico prints from Ely & Walker, and patterns and quilting supplies from Yours Truly. Eventually, Prairie Flower Crafts took over the entire area. Sara retired in 2013 and sold the store to Paula Royer, a former employee and Alden resident.

The store has rooms brimming with fabric, notions, and quilting supplies. Quilters come from near and far for the outstanding selection of material and the personalized service they receive. If you love fabric, this is a shop you will want to visit.

# Stitches Quilt Shop

Another quilt shop we visit often is Stitches Quilt Shop, in McPherson Kansas. Janet's love for quilting is expressed in her stunning displays of fabrics and quilts that fill the shop. Whether you are a beginner or an accomplished quilter, she is always willing to help you find the perfect fabrics for a beautiful handmade quilt.

The shop features an extensive selection of gorgeous 100% cotton fabric, including flannels and wide backing. Sewing notions, books, and the latest techniques are displayed throughout the store. Classes are offered routinely and are usually filled. As you design your next project, make plans to visit Stitches Quilt Shop.

# Guests

We have also invited a number of guests into our homes including Kathy Schmidt and Ruth Goertzen, who live in our local community. Both are avid quilters and have designed and pieced numerous quilts of all sizes as well as wall hangings. After seeing their personal quilts and hearing their stories, we were enticed to try new techniques and different patterns.

Mickie Watson is the owner of the Wooly Red Hen located near Hillsboro, Kansas. Her small shop includes an assortment of handcrafted items such as soft sculpture primitive animals, hand-poured candles, and consignment articles from area artisans. She also offers picture matting and framing. She works closely with each customer. Mickie enjoys sharing her craftsmanship. As a guest of our group, she offered a fun-filled evening as we learned how to create unique Christmas garland.

# Taste of Home Cooking School

Never underestimate the possibilities of fun while learning something new about cooking. Especially when you are sitting in the front row and your group has somehow drawn the attention of the culinary specialist providing the program.

In 2011, The Taste of Home Cooking School came to Bethel College Campus in North Newton, Kansas. The school provided an entertaining two-hour cooking demonstration. A culinary specialist provided step-by-step instructions for numerous appealing recipes.

Everyone in attendance received a gift bag filled with goodies. Attendees could register for door prizes, which included the finished dishes created that evening.

Although none of us won a dish, we were rewarded with an assortment of other prizes, which included a number of Taste of Home magazines. Having recipes in hand, we decided to choose six different dishes and make them for a meal for our next meeting. Dishes included Ground Nut Stew, Cheddar Soda Bread, Fruit Salad, Cranberry Turkey Crostini, Salad with Pork Strips, and a luscious Turtle Pecan Cheesecake. Although the presentation of our recipes may not have been as flamboyant, they were quite tasty.

Several different snack mix recipes were also demonstrated at the cooking school. Intrigued by the idea of trying new snack mixes, we decided to do a snack mix exchange the following Christmas. The snack mixes we exchanged included Crispix® Cheesy Crunch Mix, Chex® PB and Chocolate Blast, Crispix® Mix S'MORES, Chex® Caramel Chocolate Drizzles, Chex® Pumpkin Pie Crunch, and Hot Buttered Rum Chex®

Ground Nut Stew,
Cheddar Soda Bread,
Fruit Salad, Cranberry Turkey Cro
Salad with Pork Strips,
Turtle Pecan Cheesecake

# afternoon tea

"There are few hours in life more agreeable than the hour dedicated to the ceremony known as afternoon tea."

—Henry James

# Tea and Trunk Show

"There are few hours in life more agreeable than the hour dedicated to the ceremony known as afternoon tea." –*Henry James*, The Portrait of a Lady.

Our group is always looking for new ways to experience creativity. Kim Funk, an avid quilter in our community, provided us with just that experience. We were privileged to spend one afternoon at her house.

A tea table featured three teapots and provided us with an assortment of flavorful teas that included Papaya Black Tea, Chai Spice Black Tea, and Passion Fruit. Each of us was given a tea coaster that Kim had made from scrap fabric.

Kim and her granddaughter, Tayler, prepared an assortment of delightful pastries. While we waited, we were tempted by the Almond Cream Strawberries and a Lemon Trifle Custard.

After tea, we were treated to a trunk show that included about twenty-five quilts. Kim had quilted most of these quilts. The others were antique quilts she had purchased or had been given.

Kim started quilting in 1974 and hasn't stopped. An assortment of pieced quilts she designed and made for a particular purpose are scattered throughout her home.

She designed a quilt for each of her children and grandchildren to celebrate their birth. An I Spy quilt lays ready when the younger grandchildren come for a visit.

Her hands have created and pieced together five quilts that were donated to the Kansas Mennonite Relief Sale. She was privileged to have her mother cross-stitch blocks for one of these quilts and have her mother-in-law do the hand-quilting.

Through these quilts for MCC Kim has shared her passion for quilting while touching the lives of countless people in many different countries.

Henry James was correct. Those two hours we dedicated to an afternoon tea on a hot summer day were most agreeable.

# LEMON CUSTARD TRIFLE

INGREDIENTS:
8 ounces cream cheese, room temperature
4 tablespoons lemon juice
10 ounces sweetened condensed milk
1 teaspoon vanilla extract
1 lemon cake mix

DIRECTIONS:
Bake the lemon cake according to directions on the box and allow to cool. Beat the cream cheese until creamy.

Gradually beat in the sweetened condensed milk. Add the lemon juice and vanilla.

Cut the cake into bite-size pieces.

In a custard glass place one layer of lemon cake, followed by a layer of custard, then a layer of blueberries. Add a layer of whipped cream and top with pieces of kiwi and whole strawberries.

*afternoon tea*

# BUTTER HORNS

INGREDIENTS:
2 sticks of margarine
1 12 ounce container of small curd cottage cheese
2 cups flour

DIRECTIONS:
In a small bowl cream the margarine and cottage cheese. Then add the flour.
Divide the dough into 3 or 4 balls. Roll each ball into a 10-12 inch circle.
Cut into 8 or 12 wedges. Roll the wedges starting at the wide end.

Bake at 350° for 30-40 minutes.

Glaze:
2 tablespoons butter, melted
2 tablespoons half and half
1 teaspoon vanilla

Mix ingredients and add enough powdered sugar to make a thin frosting.

Butter Horns can be filled with jelly, fruits, cinnamon and sugar, or
chopped pecans.

*Pattern: Scrappy Quilt*
*Quilt Maker: Dora Goerzen*

# OUR HANDS ARE RENEWED

*"But those who hope in the Lord shall renew their strength."* — *Isaiah 40:31 (NIV)*

## Maple Memories

Taking time to rest and relax is essential for emotional and spiritual health. Even Jesus needed time to rejuvenate. In Mark 6, verse 31, he encourages the disciples to come to a quiet place and rest.

It is important for us to sometimes step away from our usual routine. We need to spend time with people who lift us up, support our values, laugh with us, and listen to our needs. It is when we allow ourselves these opportunities that we are rejuvenated and our strength is restored.

Maple Memories Craft House in McPherson Kansas has provided this sanctuary for our small group. The house, built in 1905 is a two-story house with five bedrooms upstairs; they include 12 twin beds. Spacious rooms allow guests to do a variety of crafting. Other rooms invite people to sit back and enjoy the moment. A kitchen and dining room provide an area for guests to share a meal together.

Once a year, usually in March, we rent this beautiful old home for a day. In this environment, we find time to relax, unwind, and begin and complete projects.

## CRAFTING AND CREATING

One year we chose to do group projects. Ilona taught us how to use felted wool to make embellished pin cushions. The pattern we used was My Favorite Pincushion Pattern, by Darcy Ashton. We enjoyed the opportunity to create something entirely different.

*"I enjoyed this because it was my first time to craft with wool."* —Sharon

Sharon showed us a quick and easy way to make a table runner. We didn't have time to finish our runners that day, so most of us completed them later. At a meeting two years later, Sharon confessed she still had this project in her UFO (unfinished object) pile.

Those of us who did finish the runners used them in our homes, or gave them as gifts.

*Bonus: The cushion is stuffed with crushed black walnuts, which make pins slide in more easily.*

When attending a quilting retreat, Lois learned how to make a Snap Happy Bag. It can be used to hold small items such as sewing and quilting supplies. With excellent instructions, we were all able to complete the snap bags that day. These were fun to make, and our choices of fabrics created six different unique bags.

Each year brings with it the opportunity to share and learn from each other. Friendships are a wonderful gift from God. Texture and vivid colors draw us to the fabric, but it is the thread that holds the quilt together. Likewise, as individuals we are drawn to each other for many different reasons. But it is the honesty, encouragement, and support that nourish our souls and bind our lives together.

*It is called a Snap Happy Bag because a section of a rigid tape measure is sewn into the top for the closing mechanism.*

# BUTTERFINGER PIE

A key ingredient to most any gathering is food. Planning for our day at Maple Memories includes preparing a menu for lunch. Each person volunteers to prepare an item. Each year's menu features something new.

Whether it's the aroma of a spicy taco soup or a wedge of melt-in- your mouth pie, food draws us together and invites us to relate to each other.

— *Menu* —

*Sharon's Chicken Salad*

*Crusty Rolls*

*Fresh Fruit Salad*

*Butterfinger Pie*

Makes one 9 inch pie
FILLING:
8 ounces cream cheese
½ cup creamy peanut butter
8 fun-size Butterfinger Candy Bars

Pinch of salt
8 ounces of Cool Whip
¼ cup of sugar

TOPPING:
4 ounces Cool Whip
Chocolate syrup
2 Fun Size Butterfinger candy bars

Make your favorite pie crust and bake it. Let it cool.

For the filling, beat together the cream cheese, peanut butter, sugar, and salt on medium speed until light and fluffy, about 3 minutes. Using a rubber spatula, fold in half of the Cool Whip until completely combined, and then fold in the chopped Butterfinger candy bars. Pour filling into the prebaked crust and smooth into an even layer. Top with the remaining 4 ounces of Cool Whip, then refrigerate for at least 1 hour.

Before serving, drizzle with chocolate syrup and top with additional chopped Butterfinger candy bars.

# SHARON'S CHICKEN SALAD

INGREDIENTS:
2 13 ounce cans white meat chicken
½ teaspoon salt
½ cup sour cream
½ cup light Miracle Whip
2 tablespoons sugar
1 cup red grapes, halved
½ cup chopped walnuts

DIRECTIONS:
Use fork to break the chicken apart. Add the rest of ingredients and mix (adjust ingredient amounts to personal taste). Chill the mixture. Serve on croissants or bread of your choosing.

*This chicken salad is easy to make. The red grapes add a splash of color to the dish plus provide a bit of tanginess to the flavor, while the walnuts add just the right amount of crunchiness.*

—Sharon Unruh

Pattern: Grandmother's Flower Garden
Quilt Maker: Mary Voth, mother of Darlene Schroeder

# OUR HANDS TREASURE

*For where your treasure is, there will your heart be also.* —*Matthew 6:21 (NIV)*

Some people want only the best, the newest, and the brightest. Others, however, enjoy the thrill of rummaging through antique shops looking for items that others have discarded.

Antique shops can be the ideal place to dig around and find the ultimate treasure. Some offer overpriced items that may have no value to you but may have great value for someone else.

Meandering through an antique shop, one ponders what stories the items could tell. Would the story be of elegance boasting of glamour, or might it be filled with mystery and suspense? Perhaps it would tell a story of an ordinary life, a life filled with hard work, compassion for others, and a heart overflowing with love.

What then is the significance of something old? To some, an antique item may represent the continuity of life. It may generate a desire to know something about what came before us. Perhaps it is a way we respect something that has stood the test of time.

Our group has visited a number of antique shops. One balmy spring day we made our way to Abilene, Kansas and wandered through shops filled with an assortment of relics from the past. We found and purchased various items. One individual found a wooden high chair reminiscent of her childhood and now is just the perfect fit for her granddaughter.

All of us own items that have been passed down from generation to generation. A beautiful handmade wooden cradle, made by hand, awaiting the birth of a child. Dolls nestled in worn-out blankets that show the everyday play of a small child. A long white, christening dress gracefully displayed, reminding us of someone's commitment to raising their child in the church. Intricate hand-work done by hands in Greece now displayed on a coffee table in Kansas remind us of someone back home. Beautiful handmade quilts tenderly stitched by the light of a kerosene lamp on a winter evening. All of these are just a sampling of the treasures we have come to value.

Many people truly appreciate the items passed down to them. Others dream of acquiring the one item that will make them rich or bring them happiness. Of course, material possessions are just that, articles that bring pleasure for a short period. The real treasures of life include the laughter we share with family, the smile of a child or the cup of coffee shared with a group of friends. These are the genuine treasures, the greatest picks of all.

In traditional Greek culture, a bride often had a dowry. Creating a dowry was an essential part of a young girl's training. While building her dowry, she obtained the necessary skills she would use later. A dowry consisted mostly of linens made by the bride and the women of her family. Typical items included towels, sheets, table linens, blankets, pillowcases, tablecloths, doilies, and other necessities. Many of the items were decorated with intricate embroidery.

While I was growing up, young girls still followed this practice. Usually, a girl's mother would start the dowry, and then the girl would add to it. Since my mother had passed away, I began my own. Later, I added to the dowry by purchasing linens from other people.

My mother created her dowry in the 1930s, as she prepared for her marriage. Among the items in her dowry was a thick, 100% wool blanket. This blanket was made from scratch. My mother and her mother would

have helped shear the sheep. Then the wool was washed and laid out to dry. Next, the wool was carded and spun into thread. To obtain the right color they might have purchased a dye or made their own. Finally, she would have used a loom to create the blanket.

This blanket is one of the items my mother chose to save for me. I gave away many of the items in my dowry when I married and moved with my husband to Kansas. In remembrance of my mother, I chose to bring this treasured blanket with me to start a new life in a very different culture.

—Dora Goerzen

# OUR HANDS CREATE

*Each one should use whatever gift he has received to serve others faithfully administering God's grace in its various forms.*

—I Peter 4: 10 (NIV)

God has given us a variety of gifts and expects us to use them in creative ways. The word create is mentioned numerous times throughout the Bible. In Genesis we read about the creation of the world. Later in Exodus 31, God tells Moses he has given Bezalel, son of Uri, the skills and expertise to create artistic designs in gold, silver, and bronze. These designs plus others would be used to embellish the tent.

God's conversation with Moses helps us understand that God not only appreciates those who are skillful and use their gifts, but also that he is the source of these gifts. There are numerous ways that we can use our skills and creativity to glorify God.

All six of us use our hands to create and stitch quilts, which have been made from fabrics that were chosen specifically for particular projects. God also challenges us to seek out those gifts that may not be as obvious. As we accept those challenges, we allow ourselves a second chance to experience an opportunity we may have missed. When we surround ourselves with people who support and encourage us, we can overcome our uncertainties and begin to use these new gifts to serve others.

All of us, whether we are teachers, artists, musicians, quilters, gardeners or authors, have a mutual mission. First, we must recognize the value of the gift and then understand how we can use that gift to glorify God. It is with this recognition that we bring meaning to our lives and become a valuable part of God's plan here on earth.

My mother was a seamstress. With five daughters, there was always plenty of sewing to do. Many times she would use feed sack material to create colorful, but practical dresses for us to wear. If she wasn't sewing clothing for her family, she was busy quilting. A quilt would be set up in the dining room, and soon several other neighbor ladies and friends would gather for an afternoon of quilting and visiting.

One year when I was at home with the mumps, my mom let me use the sewing machine. This was the start of many needle and thread projects. I sewed countless doll clothes and many years later I sewed my wedding dress. I remember the overwhelming feeling of cutting into the beautiful white fabric and hoping it would be as attractive as I had imagined it to be.

When our daughters were born, and I was working away from home, it seemed there was little time for sewing. Eventually, time became more available, and once again my hands began to create a variety of projects.

My first quilt was a pattern I designed. Later, I started piecing another quilt, which focused on early 1900s fabric pictures. These pictures were framed within the quilt. When I took the quilt to have it machine-quilted, I was told I had made a blended quilt. At the time, I didn't even know what a blended quilt was.

Now I have completed quilts for my two daughters and five grandsons. At one time, I made a Grandmothers Flower Garden quilt. This quilt is comprised of numerous small hexagons. Wanting to try something different, I pieced all the hexagons by hand and then used my old treadle sewing machine to stitch it together.

I have always enjoyed working with color and designs. I find that quilting gives me the opportunity to express my creativity while forming a beautiful piece of art.

—Darlene Schroeder

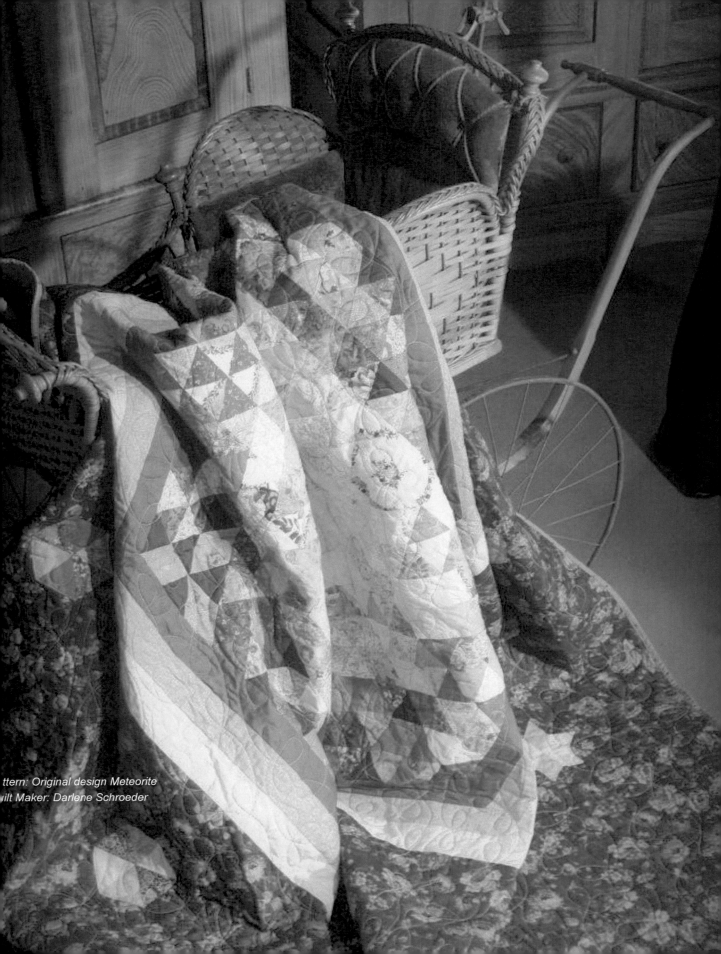

Sewing has always been part of my life. My mother owned an old treadle Singer sewing machine that I used to learn how to sew. It seems the machine was always open, except on Sundays when we put everything away.

When I was in grade school, I joined 4-H and enrolled in sewing. We sewed aprons, tea towels, and simple garments. I remember spending time removing stitches when it wasn't sewn correctly and being frustrated! These garments were exhibited at the Turner County Fair, and I always looked forward to receiving ribbons and reading the judges' comments.

During sewing class in high school, I stitched garments such as skirts and shirts, and my sewing skills began to improve. I have always enjoyed handwork such as cross-stitch embroidery and embroidered quilt blocks. At one time, I did a lot of counted cross-stitch but found the tiny stitches were hard on my eyes.

When I got older, I became more interested in piecing quilts. Eventually, I pieced my first quilt, Ohio Star using three different fabrics. It was trial and error, and I decided I needed to learn more about quilting.

When a Block of the Month class was offered at a local quilt shop, I enrolled and took a twelve-month course entitled "Egg Money Quilts" by Eleanor Burns. I sewed a 1930s vintage sampler with twelve inch size blocks. Each block was sewn from 1930s reproduction vintage fabrics. Many quilts from the 1930s were made from flour and chicken feed sacks. I used various templates and soon discovered how to piece a variety of patterns. My finished quilt was quilted by an excellent hand-quilter in our local community.

Each time I piece another quilt I enjoy quilting more. Even though I sometimes need to take out stitches and start over. Today, I don't receive ribbons or comments from a judge, but instead have the satisfaction of knowing I have completed a beautiful quilt with my hands.

—Lynne Voth

Pattern: Egg MoneyQuilts, Eleanor Burns
Quilt Maker: Lynne Voth

My mom, like many others, was a great seamstress. Sewing was done more as a necessity than for enjoyment. She created adorable dresses embellished with smocking across the top just for me. These were my favorites.

One Sunday when I was three or four years old, I was wearing one of those smocked dresses. My parents were getting ready for evening church, and I was getting impatient. While waiting I decided to go outside and check on the cows. Being curious, I leaned over a two-foot high tank full of water and promptly fell in. As I stood up, I saw my parents running out of the house. Of course, I was reprimanded for being near the tank. As the story was retold throughout the years, it seemed my mom was most concerned about whether the smocked dress had been ruined.

I never saw my mom piece quilts, but she did quilt whole cloth quilts. I learned the basics of sewing while taking Home Economics in high school. I also enjoyed sewing clothing for my children when they were young. I remember the challenge of sewing two different suits for one of my small boys who was asked to be a ring bearer at a relative's wedding. Interestingly enough, I even made matching bow ties. Having two girls gave me the opportunity to sew dresses filled with ruffles and lace plus doll blankets and colorful pillows. Now I receive enjoyment by sewing some of these items for my granddaughters.

My mother-in-law helped me make quilts for three of my four children. She showed me how to cut the blocks from double knit and put the blocks together to form a pattern or to make a scrappy quilt using all different colors and patterns of fabric. When the quilt was pieced, she taught me how to put it in a quilting frame in our basement. We spent many hours tying the quilt while my children played contently under the quilt in the frame.

Later, I became interested in appliqué. A friend and I began marketing our appliqué creations at local arts and craft fairs, after refining our skills. For a number of years I also hosted a Christmas open house where our products and other artists' products were for sale.

I have always appreciated the beauty of quilts, especially the older ones. Obtaining just the right fabric to complement a pattern I saw made me recognize that I, too, could create a quilt. Meeting once a month with friends who also enjoy quilting has inspired and encouraged me to try larger and more complicated patterns and designs. Along with the gratification of crafting a beautiful quilt, I have also found quilting to be very therapeutic.

—Sharon Unruh

ern: Turning Twenty, Trisha Cribbs
Maker: Sharon Unruh

One might define quilting in a number of ways. It could be the process of piecing fabric together to create a design, or it might refer to the method of stitching several layers of fabric and batting with a machine or by hand.

My mom made "whole cloth" quilts, by hand, but never pieced. This was a skill I also learned. It wasn't until much later that I began to explore the idea of cutting and piecing a quilt.

While growing up, I watched her fingers carefully as she nimbly pushed the needle back and forth, crafting just the right design for an expectant mother. Quilting was something that brought great pleasure to my mom. She began by asking expectant mothers what colors of fabric they would like, and then would painstakingly draw a design on the top of a quilt after it was stretched on a frame. Sometimes she would quilt late in the evening after the many chores of the day were done.

As I grew older and more interested in quilting, I was taught how to hand-quilt. My beginning stitches were large and uneven, but eventually my fingers began to understand the rhythm of hand quilting.

Shortly after our daughter was born, I decided to try to make a quilt of my own. Choosing to design and quilt a whole-cloth king-sized quilt may not have been the best starter project. But with my mom's help, I pinned it on the frame, marked it and finally began quilting! Although I enjoyed the process of quilting, I soon realized this project was a huge one. Occasionally my mom would come and spend a few hours and quilt alongside me, and one afternoon four of my paternal aunts came and helped me quilt. Eventually, after many hours of work, the quilt was completed. A lady hemstitched around the edges, and then my mom crocheted the border.

Since then I have hand-quilted a number of other whole-cloth quilts and always enjoy seeing the pattern come to life as I stitch. In recent years I have also enjoyed learning more about the art of piecing fabric, and have completed a number of pieced projects.

Now, when I piece or stitch a quilt, I am reminded of my mom's fingers fluidly sliding the needle through the fabric. I cherish the memory of learning to quilt from her and our time spent together.

—Ilona Abrahams

*rn: Whole Cloth Quilt*
*Maker: Ilona Abrahams*

For a period of my life, I lived with my godmother in Greece. She was a great seamstress for the neighborhood and although she did teach me to hand-stitch, embroider and do some basic repairs on clothing, I was never taught to use the sewing machine. I think my godmother may have been afraid I would break the sewing machine because she never let me use it!

Soon after I came to Kansas, my mother-in-law gave me an older sewing machine. Although it worked well, it seemed too complicated to learn. So consequently I didn't use it very much. My curiosity about quilting began after I met my good friend Wilma Schmidt who owned a small quilt shop in North Newton, Kansas. When I visited the shop, I always admired the quilts she had on display. Occasionally the store offered classes, and eventually she persuaded me to take a class.

Now, operating the old sewing machine became a reality. After finally figuring out how to thread the machine, I began to practice sewing straight lines. I soon realized it was going to be much harder than it appeared. There were many days when I stared at the machine and thought it was the devil. Sometimes I was so frustrated I contemplated kicking the machine out of the house. Finally, after a lot of practice, I began to feel more confident.

Next, I was determined to create a quilt for each of my children. I selected the pattern Double Irish Chain for my first quilt. As I began to piece the blocks together, I soon began to appreciate how quilting was like putting together a puzzle. Soon, I looked forward to sitting down in front of The Beast and was excited when I finally finished my first quilt. In fact, I was so ecstatic when I was done that I celebrated in Greek fashion with a glass of wine!

I continued to quilt, but when I entered the workforce, it was difficult to find time for my new hobby. It wasn't until I retired that I was able to focus on quilting again. Now, I find joy in choosing vibrant fabric and appealing patterns to create beautiful quilts. As for The Beast, it is now used as intended, and is not just as a piece of furniture located in the corner of a room.

—Dora Goerzen

Pattern: *Double Irish Chain*
Quilt Maker: *Dora Goerzen*

Quilting has been a part of my life for as long as I can remember. It seemed my grandmother always had a quilt or comforter in the frame. She enjoyed collecting denim strips and other fabric scraps. After she had cut them into squares, she would piece them together to make quilts or comforters. Some of these would be hand-quilted while others were tied. Finished quilts were given to MCC or another relief organization. Since everything was hand-quilted, my mom and aunts would often spend the day quilting at her house.

I also observed my mother quilt when she met with other ladies at the church. The women were members of the Junior Mission Circle and gathered together twice a month to quilt. Usually they made five to ten quilts a year. Every year they had a mission sale, and the proceeds would go to a designated mission project.

After having so many mentors, I decided it was time to make my own comforter. Using double knit fabric, I pieced together two twin-sized comforters that I tied rather than quilted.

In the early 1980s, I took my first quilting class with a friend. At this class, we learned how to strip quilt. Later, I used this method and made quilts for both of my girls. My mother and I hand-quilted both of these quilts.

When my grandparents celebrated their fiftheth wedding anniversary, my mother and her sisters-in-law decided to make a family tree heirloom quilt top for them and then asked my grandmother to help them hand-quilt it. Some years later, when my parents started to plan their own fiftieth anniversary, my sisters and sisters-in-law decided we wanted to do the same thing for them. After some planning, I drew a design, and we began cutting and piecing a Log Cabin-style quilt. To work on the quilt, we planned a three-day holiday retreat at my sister's home where we finished the quilt top. Eventually, when all the names and dates were on it, we showed it to our parents, and asked Mother to help us quilt it. When my parents' belongings were divided, I inherited this quilt.

A new tradition started when we decided to make a quilt as a wedding gift for each of the nineteen grandchildren. So far, we have made fourteen quilts. Each couple gets to pick their colors, fabric, and how they want it arranged. We spend one long weekend piecing the top and tying it. The mother of the grandchild attaches the binding to finish the quilt.

My interest in quilting continues. Just like my grandmother and mother, whose hands were always busy quilting, I too enjoy the challenge of finding the right fabric for my next quilt project. Seeing how the pattern and colors blend reminds me of the value of family and the memories we have created.

—Lois Voth

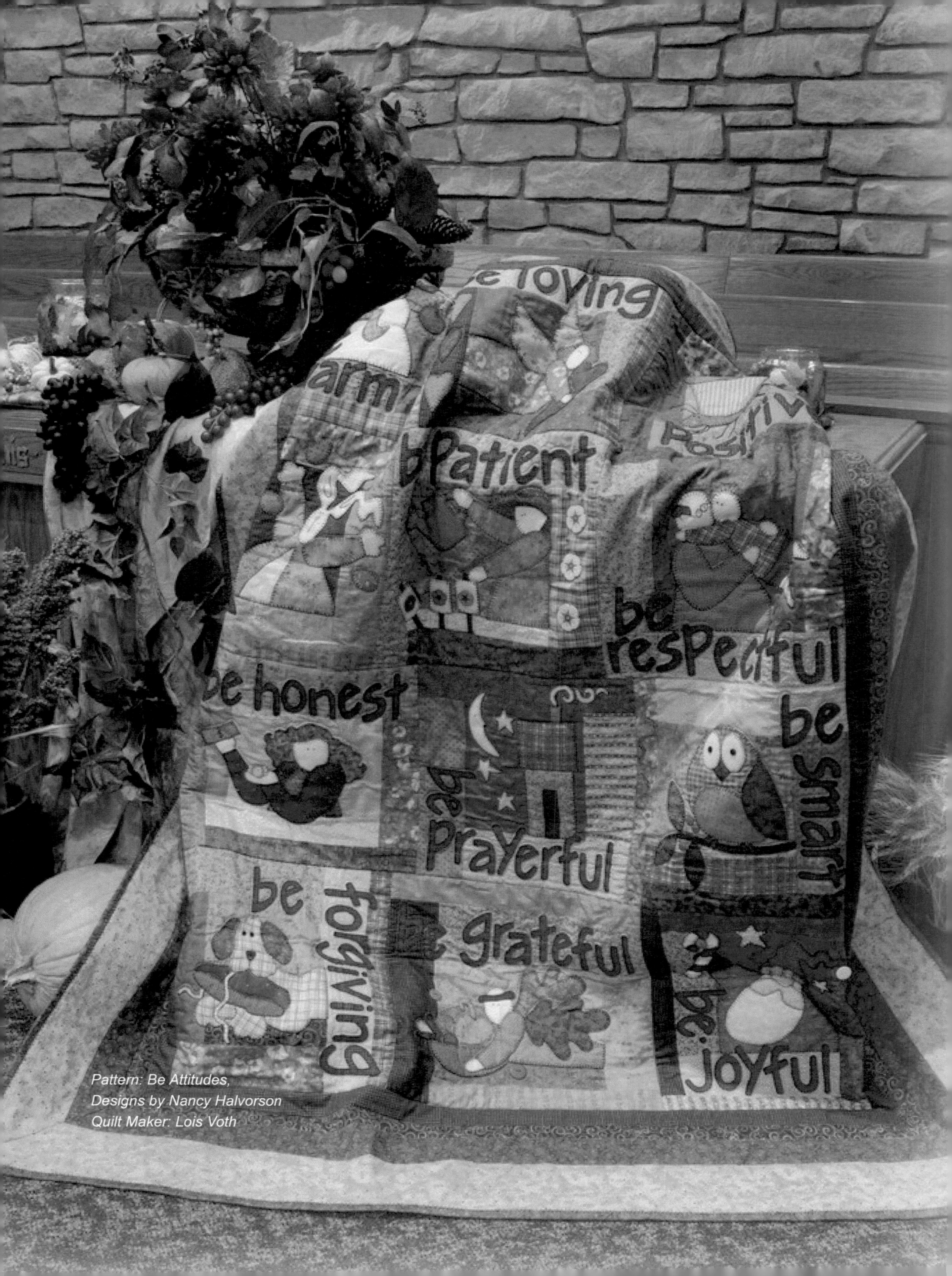

be loving

warm

be patient

positive

be respectful

be honest

be smart

be prayerful

be forgiving

grateful

joyful

Pattern: Yellow Brick Road
Atkinson Designs
Quilt Maker: Lynne Voth

# OUR HANDS SERVE

*God is not unjust; he will not forget your work and the love you have shown him as you have helped his people and continue to help them.*
—Hebrew 6:10 (NIV)

Walk into any restaurant, and someone is waiting to serve you. Being waited on is something we enjoy. Waiters and waitresses make sure your beverage glass is constantly full, and the food you ordered is to your liking.

As much as we appreciate being served, it is equally important for us to serve others. God reminds us it is not how many people serve us, but instead how many people we serve. We need to take the initiative to serve others. As we serve, we take notice of those who need our assistance. In Exodus chapter 3, a burning bush grabs Moses' attention. When God comes to Moses and asks him to lead the Israelites, he responds with, "Who, me?" Moses continues by offering many excuses as to why he is not a worthy candidate to lead the people. It is only after an extended conversation with God that Moses is convinced he can do what God is asking him to do.

Our lives are filled from sun-up to sundown with various obligations. Throughout this busyness, how do we go about the task of serving others? It is essential to stop trying to work God into our schedules, but instead work our schedules around him. In Matthew, chapter 20, Jesus calls Peter and Andrew to follow him. In verse 20, it says, "They immediately left their nets and followed him." They didn't question Jesus. They didn't tell him to come back the next day; they simply went.

God's intention for us is to have the heart of a servant. Just as in the story of Moses, God may ask us to serve in ways that make us uncomfortable and, therefore, reluctant. Throughout the Bible, Jesus hangs out with the last and the least to show us how to serve. We can prepare ourselves to serve through honest and meaningful conversation with God. It is important to humble ourselves, serve where most required, and seek those opportunities that reflect a genuine need. It is through this process we can respond faithfully to God's invitation to be missional people. It is when we serve with a joyful heart that others can see Christ.

Our group continues to look for ways to serve others, either individually or as a group. Many of us have been involved in the Kansas Mennonite Relief Sale, held annually at the Kansas State Fairground in Hutchinson, Kansas. This event that started 47 years ago, raises about $500,000 a year for Mennonite Central Committee. Proceeds from the sale help fight world hunger and provide hope to people in need. This annual event is orchestrated by 70 Mennonite, Brethren in Christ, and Amish congregations. The benefit auctions include a variety of items, including antique cars and tractors. Tantalizing aromas of ethnic foods pervades the air.

One of the auctions is devoted primarily to handmade quilts. Members of our group have contributed quilts, table runners, or other items. Collaborating with one another and producing a quilt that will be sold for the benefit of others allows us to use our gifts that God has given us.

The MCC sale is known for its delicious ethnic foods. Throughout the years, many of us have also been involved in food preparation. We have helped prepare German sausage, made zwieback and created delicious pies. Some of us have worked on food committees or have helped serve food at different locations. A German buffet serves 6,000-10,000 people. People wait in long lines for their turn to choose from ethnic favorites such as verenika, bohne beroggi, borscht, cherry moos, zwiebach, and pie.

Verenika is perhaps one of the most unusual items on the buffet line. Verenika is a dumpling filled with seasoned cottage cheese and served with a rich ham gravy. Mennonites originating from South Russia brought this recipe with them when they migrated to Kansas in 1874. The recipe that follows has been passed down from some of our relatives.

*Pattern: Take Five by Accuquilt*
*Quilt Makers: Lois Voth and*
*Sharon Unruh*

People all over the world look for resourceful ways to serve others. Greek individuals are no different. Many more holidays are celebrated in Greece than in America. Honoring particular saints is the focus of many holidays. Catholic churches hold sales with the proceeds being donated to the poor, to celebrate some of these holidays. Parishioners will bring baked goods and handmade items, such as doilies, to sell. People come from throughout the larger cities to buy and support these efforts.

# VERENIKA

## DOUGH FOR VERENIKA
2½ cups sifted all-purpose flour
1 teaspoon salt
3 egg whites
½ cup milk
½ cup half-and-half

## COTTAGE CHEESE FILLING
2½ cups dry or bakers' cottage cheese
3 egg yolks
½ teaspoon salt
1 teaspoon minced onion

## DIRECTIONS:
In a deep bowl combine flour and salt. Make a well in the center. Add egg whites and liquid. Knead together. Turn out onto floured board and knead until dough is smooth. Too much kneading can toughen dough. Divide into two pieces. Cover and let stand in the refrigerator for several hours.

Prepare the cottage cheese filling. Roll the dough very thin on a lightly floured board. Cut 3-inch round circles. Place a spoonful of filling in the center. Moisten the edges with water and pinch together to form a seal.

Some people prefer to fry the verenika in hot oil. Others boil them in salted water. If boiling them, drop them into boiling salted water. Stir gently so they do not stick to the bottom of the pan. Boil for 3-4 minutes. Remove and drain in a colander. At this point some people prefer to brown them in a small amount of hot butter.

Many people prefer eating them with rich ham gravy while others pour dark syrup over the top. The recipe for ham gravy is listed below.

## HAM GRAVY
In a skillet sauté two tablespoons margarine and one finely chopped small onion.
Add 1 cup cream and salt and pepper to taste.
Add 1 cup cubed ham and simmer.

*Pattern: Tumbler Quilt, Original Design*
*Quilt Maker: Sharon Unruh*

# OUR HANDS EMBRACE

*So then, brothers, stand firm and hold to the teachings we passed on to you, whether by word of mouth or letter.*

*—2 Thessalonians 2:15 (NIV)*

Family stories not only link us to the past, but they also knit our families together. They help us identify who we are and what is significant in our life. We take pleasure in retelling these stories to each new generation.

As we hear and convey the stories, traditions begin to emerge in our families. Some traditions require more work than others. Some are forgotten and are cast aside as new ones start to take shape. Even so, all have a purpose. These traditions become a fragment of our life; they help tell the story. Traditions help generations connect and give people a sense of belonging and acceptance. As time passes, they become threads that weave the family together. Traditions help us reflect on the past, define the present, and influence the future. It is essential to provide a solid foundation for future generations.

What are your family traditions? Perhaps it is a family reunion that takes place once a year. A favorite ethnic recipe becomes a tradition after it is repeatedly made and is passed down to the next generation. Holidays provide the perfect occasion for stories to be told and traditions to be created. As we study old photos that have been handed down, we see faith and wisdom etched on the faces, and we desire to emulate their lives.

God gives us the opportunity to cultivate the seeds that have been planted by people who have gone before us. Parents and grandparents have passed the teachings of Christ to us. As Christians, it is important to pass along this message. Through this process, we can reach out and embrace the teaching of God and invite him into our life.

W affles and sauce. What do they have to do with Christmas? I'm not sure when Christmas and waffles and sweet white sauce joined hands, but for our family, they are a couple.

Our family usually gathers together on Christmas Eve for an early evening meal. A simple meal of waffles and sauce and sometimes German sausage helps us celebrate the birth of Jesus. Several area churches still host Christmas Eve services. It has become our tradition to have a meal together and then attend a Christmas Eve service, as a family, at a local church.

Years ago when one of our daughters and her husband lived out of state and were not able to come home for Christmas, we called them while eating our waffles and sauce. We discovered that even though there was a difference in time zones, we were all eating waffles and sauce at the same time on Christmas Eve.

Traditionally, waffles were made in most Mennonite households, sometimes served as a dessert but also eaten as the main meal. Jerry and I both grew up eating waffles and sauce as a meal. Each Christmas Eve we are reminded of our Mennonite heritage and are blessed to be able to share this with our children and grandchildren.
—Darlene Schroeder

## WHITE SAUCE

INGREDIENTS:
2 cups milk
3 tablespoons cornstarch
½ cup sugar
1 teaspoon vanilla

DIRECTIONS:
Heat 2 cups milk. While this mixture is heating make a batter using the sugar, cornstarch and vanilla. Slowly add this mixture to the heated milk. Continue to stir until mixture begins to boil and thicken. For a richer sauce you can use 1 cup milk and 1 cup cream.

Recipe originally published in Christian Home Cookbook, copyright© 1967 by Gospel Publishers, Hesston Kansas.

I grew up a farmer's daughter. My father was a custom harvester and followed the harvest all summer. Following the harvest meant beginning at home in Oklahoma, then proceeding through Kansas, Colorado, Nebraska, South Dakota, and finally finishing in North Dakota. My father's first year to follow the harvest was in 1950, and he continued until 1993.

When my brothers and sisters and I were young, Dad hired four to six college-age boys to help with the harvest. The entire family traveled and lived in camper trailers all summer. We were usually gone from the end of May through Labor Day. Some years my mom came home early so we could get ready for school. As my brothers got older, they began to help more. By 1983 it had become a family affair when my brothers and two sisters began to help and take along their families.

Interestingly enough, I married a farmer. Even though we are small farmers, our family has also always been involved. We may not do custom harvesting, but we are wheat farmers who are dependent on the weather and the good Lord. When it was time to take wheat to the elevator, our two girls always enjoyed the trip to the elevator with me or their Grandpa Voth. Whether it was noon or evening, we all looked forward to my mother-in-law bringing a delicious meal out to the wheat field.

Today our daughters and son-in-law also participate. Everyone contributes in some way, whether that means running the combine, taking a load of wheat into town or preparing a well-deserved meal. Carrying on the tradition is important. In 2013, our four-month-old granddaughter had her initial combine ride and took her first trip to the elevator.

—Lois Voth

Many years ago, my mother and I began a Christmas bake day. We set a day aside and made Christmas goodies and candy. As my brothers married, we invited their wives to become a part of this tradition. Everyone brought supplies and ingredients for the recipes they wanted to make. We enjoyed the camaraderie while the aroma of cookies and the sweetness of candy enveloped the house. Only the ladies were allowed to participate. When the granddaughters grew older, they also joined the fun. Earlier in the day, Mom would make a huge pot of chili and put a dish of hot burgers in the oven to bake. This meal would be ready by the time we were done baking, and then the men and the boys would join us for supper. Fellowship, food, and fun, made for many memories.

As the family continued to grow, we were unable to carry on this arrangement. Not willing to give up this tradition however, I began doing the same thing with my daughters, daughter-in-law, and my mom. As my five granddaughters turn eight they are also included in the fun. We continue to meet on a Saturday in December. Although we use some of the same recipes each year, we also try to add some new ones. Peppernuts, Mexican wedding cakes, and sugar cookies are a few of our favorites. Although my mom has passed away, she is there in spirit.

God reminds us to take time for each other during the frenzy of the Christmas season. As we sit down with friends and share these homemade goodies, we understand how traditions can help us experience the real joy of Christmas.

—Sharon Unruh

## HOT BURGERS (baked)

INGREDIENTS:

1½ pounds lean hamburger
8 saltine crackers
1½ teaspoon salt
1 large onion, grated

2 eggs
1 cup milk
1 tablespoon chili powder

DIRECTIONS:
Crush the crackers and soak in the milk. Mix all ingredients together thoroughly. Bake in 350° oven for 1 hour. Stir occasionally. Serve on hamburger buns with ketchup and cheese if desired.

In Greece, more emphasis is placed on Easter than on Christmas. Easter is based on the Julian calendar and for this reason is usually celebrated later than in the United States.

Preparations for Easter begin on Palm Sunday. In church, we make crosses out of palm branches, and everyone takes one home. Holy week begins with this activity.

Traditionally, throughout Holy Week, my family began to bake Easter sweet breads and dye eggs red. Easter eggs were dyed red to represent the blood of Christ. The shell of the egg symbolizes the resurrection and new life. On Good Friday, we began to bring wreaths of flowers and decorate the church. During this time, color in the church changes from dark to light as Holy Week progresses.

On Easter Sunday, we crack the eggs during dinner. Cracking the eggs symbolizes Christ's resurrection from the dead.

A game that we play with eggs is called Tsougrisma. Two players and red eggs are needed to play the game.

The goal of the game is to crack the other's egg. The game begins with each player holding a red egg. One player taps the end of their egg lightly against the end of the other player's egg. When one end is cracked, the winner then uses the same end of their egg to try to crack the other end of the opponent's egg. The player who successfully cracks the egg is the winner. If this sounds like Greek, it is!

I have continued this tradition with my children and grandchildren when we come together to celebrate Easter in Kansas. Even as my children and grandchildren are creating new traditions, I am blessed to be able to pass this Easter tradition on to them.

—Dora Goerzen

"Sunday morning chocolate, never heard of it," I said as my future husband attempted to explain what his mom made for breakfast every Sunday morning. A thick, rich, chocolate pudding pie with a healthy dose of meringue on top was something I could relate to, but not Sunday morning chocolate. It became apparent if I was going to make the cut and marry an Abrahams, I would need to find out more about this Sunday chocolate concoction. Because Sunday morning chocolate was a tradition at the Abrahams' house.

Sunday morning chocolate is a rich chocolate sauce that is served warm or cold over a zwieback that is slathered with butter. Hopefully, there are leftovers that can be eaten later. My first real introduction to this new dish was at an afternoon Faspa, (a light meal initially served in Mennonite homes around four in the afternoon). Everyone eagerly waited as the bowl was passed around and hoped there would be enough left for them when it got to their place at the table. Being brave and wanting to make a good appearance, I politely took a small portion. Following my fiancé's example, I broke a zwieback in half, covered it with butter, and then layered on the chocolate. As everyone watched, I chewed, swallowed, and reached for my cup of coffee to wash it down. The taste of the chocolate was wonderful, but the taste of chocolate on a zwieback was definitely an acquired taste.

As I continued to interact with my fiancé's family, I learned that this chocolate sauce recipe had been passed down from his maternal grandmother. Traditionally, it was made only on Sunday mornings, hence the name, and was always served with zwieback, which had been baked on Saturday.

After we married, I copied down the recipe and began to hone my culinary skills. Eventually, I learned how to make the chocolate sauce. Sometimes the sauce was too thin, but finally I learned how to produce a sauce that looked more like my mom-in-law's product. I still make the chocolate sauce for Sunday morning breakfast periodically. I don't usually eat it with a zwieback, but instead have found it to be an excellent dipping sauce for sliced bananas and apples.

I do not know when my husband's grandmother learned to make this sauce. But I do know that her grandchildren and great-grandchildren are now being introduced to the same delightful chocolate sauce that she taught her daughter to make.

Sunday morning chocolate has become a part of our story. Our lives are defined and shaped as we embrace traditions and pass them on to the next generation.

—Ilona Abrahams

# SUNDAY MORNING CHOCOLATE

INGREDIENTS:

1 stick oleo or butter

1½ cups white sugar

½ teaspoon vanilla

½ cup cocoa

1 – 12-ounce can evaporated milk

salt

DIRECTIONS:

Melt butter and sugar together. Add the cocoa. Then slowly add the evaporated milk. Cook until it begins to bubble and thicken. Add vanilla and a dash salt.

This will make a sauce that is not very thick. Throughout the years, I have adapted the original recipe and added one tablespoon of cornstarch to the cocoa to make a thicker sauce. This sauce can also be used as a dipping sauce for fruit as well as a delicious topping for ice cream.

As members of my family left the farm and moved to different parts of the United States, it became difficult for us to see each other.

Each Christmas we'd drive back to South Dakota and spend time with Mom and Dad. At times the weather was nasty, and the roads in Kansas, Nebraska, and South Dakota were snow-packed and icy. Often the temperatures were below freezing, and the trip became treacherous and long.

My maternal grandmother always made a special recipe of Pfeffernusse or peppernuts at Christmas. It was a very hard peppernut with sorghum syrup, spices such as fennel, anise, and black pepper. She rolled and cut penny sized cookies that were very uniform and small.

My mother continued to make this recipe, and we always looked forward to Granny's peppernuts. A number of years ago, I decided it would be fun to cut and roll peppernuts with some of my nieces who lived in the Kansas area. The first year, around Thanksgiving, everyone came to our home and brought a batch of peppernut dough. Various people have hosted the gathering since then.

After the rolling, cutting and baking, the house smells wonderful. We generally have a light meal of soup at noon and divide the cookies. Everyone always goes home with a variety of peppernuts.

We have found this is a wonderful way to reconnect and get caught up with what is going on in our lives. Each year attendance varies, but the best thing is to be together and continue the tradition of making peppernuts that Granny started so many years ago.

—Lynne Voth

Pattern: Quilt in Day, Boston Commons
Quilt Maker: Lynne Voth

*Caring Quilt*
*Designed and created by*
*Tabor Church members*

# Our Hands Receive

*Therefore I tell you, whatever you ask for in prayer, believe that you have received it, and it will be yours. —Mark 11: 24 (NIV)*

Many of us find it easier to give than to receive. As children, we eagerly looked forward with joy and wonder to receiving most anything. However, it seems we lose that as we become adults. Learning how to receive graciously needs to be a vital part of our spiritual journey. It is important to learn how to accept the opportunity to open our hearts to the giver. Many of us balk at asking for help, but when we permit ourselves to receive openly; we encourage relationships that can knit us closer together.

God invites us to find the blessings in receiving. The Bible is filled with illustrations of Jesus opening his heart and receiving a blessing in return. In Luke, chapter 7, Jesus receives a blessing when he permits a sinful woman to anoint his head with costly oil. Some who viewed this incident became angry with the woman for wasting expensive oil. Nevertheless, Jesus understood the woman's intentions and graciously received the gift. Learning how to receive is a continuous process. Throughout the years, individuals in our group have experienced many opportunities to receive blessings from others as people offered assistance, friendship, encouragement, and prayers. By willingly receiving these acts of kindness, we in turn have been filled with hope and blessed with healing. More importantly, we have allowed the giver to experience joy as we accept their gift.

Tabor Mennonite Church began to explore how they could offer healing and hope to members of the congregation who were experiencing difficulties in their lives. From this discussion, two "caring quilts" were created: one for the adults and one for the children. The center block represents the different people in the congregation, and the border of hearts signifies the congregation encircled with love and care. Two individuals from our group were instrumental in crafting this quilt. As people accept this act of kindness and wrap the quilt around them, they allow themselves to rediscover the blessings associated with receiving.

The six of us have been given the gift of supportive parents and family. They have encouraged us to enjoy the dance of life. Through example, they have instilled a deep work ethic and inspired us to discover our full potential. Mothers and grandmothers have passed down traditional recipes to help us understand our roots. Our parents taught us to have faith in ourselves and in God. With this solid foundation, we have been able to attach wings to our dreams. It is essential to give thanks for the blessings we receive, for it is when we learn how to receive that we can truly give.

Parents desire to give their children roots and wings. Roots to grow and know where they come from and wings to send them on their way. The job can be tedious and unpredictable, but it is also filled with an abundance of blessings. My parents understood this and prepared me with strong family values and morals. They provided a setting where I could learn and grow.

At an early age I learned that life isn't always fair. My life changed significantly when my dad passed away at the age of forty-eight. Now a single parent, with four children dependent on her, my mom showed me that life continued as she met each new day with hope and faith.

We are all blessed with gifts. God expects to use each of us to extend his love to others through what we do. Being able to stay home with our daughter when she was young was a real blessing. Although I enjoyed this opportunity immensely, my hands also itched to do something creative. As a child, I had always been fascinated by the elaborate wedding cakes that were displayed at weddings. After taking several cake decorating classes, I eventually opened my own professional cake decorating business in our home. This allowed me to continue to be a part of our daughter's life as well as give my hands an opportunity to create. My life was blessed by many young couples as they planned their weddings.

Later, after our daughter started school, I felt God leading me in another direction. I had always enjoyed teaching Sunday school, Bible School, and Wednesday night activities and was encouraged by family and friends to explore the possibility of returning to college. After some discernment, I realized God was waiting for me to recognize and use this gift of teaching he had given me. Now twenty years later, I have taught a multitude of kids and realize how they have enriched my life.

Life has been good, but God doesn't promise us a life without disappointments. A good friend passes away much too young, miscarriages happen, and a husband's heart attack at forty-eight, reminded me that we are not on this journey alone. Some years ago I came across this thought-provoking quote by Nouman Ali Khan. "When you are going through something hard, and you start wondering where God is, just remember the teacher is always quiet during a test." With the love of our family and friends, the prayers offered on our behalf, and our faith in God we are given the strength we need not only to survive the journey, but to LIVE IT!

—Ilona Abrahams

Plumemoos is a fruit soup made with fresh or dried fruit. Its origins date to the sixteenth century when the Dutch Mennonites lived in the Vistula Delta area in West Prussia (now Poland). The soup can be made with an assortment of fruits and is usually thickened. Originally, it was served hot or cold, as a dessert or with the main meal. Moos, once part of almost every meal, is now only occasionally cooked for a special meal, such as Christmas.

# PLUMEMOOS

IINGREDIENTS:

1½ cups raisins

1 cup sugar

1 cup prunes

DIRECTIONS:

Add enough warm water to cover the raisins and prunes. Cook until almost done. Add the sugar.

Thickening ingredients:

2 heaping tablespoons flour

2 tablespoons vinegar

Pinch of salt

1 teaspoon cinnamon

1 cup cream

Mix the thickening ingredients together and slowly add it to the first mixture. Cook until the Plumemoos begins to thicken.

Variations: Other fruits such as dried apricots can be added. Craisins can be used instead of raisins.

This original recipe comes from my husband's maternal side of the family.

—Ilona

I was raised in a farming community outside of Corn, Oklahoma. My parents instilled a deep work ethic in my three sisters, two brothers, and me. We all learned to do particular jobs and realized how working together made our jobs easier and more enjoyable. As a young teenager, I learned how to make cinnamon rolls, and my older sister was taught how to make zwieback dough. My father was a custom harvester, and we all contributed, in one way or another, to make it a successful business.

In my early twenties, I attended a program where a gentleman shared about how volunteers were needed to work with the Mennonite Central Committee. After the service, I decided to speak with the MCC representative to learn more specifics about the opportunities available. I decided to join this program and was soon given my first assignment. I spent the next two years in Akron, Pennsylvania, as a secretary. When finishing this job, I questioned where God would lead me. Having some interest in nursing and looking at some possibilities of doing an extended service job overseas, I enrolled at Eastern Mennonite College in Harrisonburg, Virginia, as a first-year nursing student. The following summer I experienced some health issues and after some discernment decided to change my major to Community Development, which was a program that combined nutrition and social work. This program seemed like a perfect fit for me.

After graduating, in May of 1980, I decided to look at some job opportunities to pay my school expenses. I was offered a job as a food service supervisor at Parkside Homes in Hillsboro, Kansas. While working at Parkside, I met some wonderful people. One of the individuals I encountered decided I should meet her son. We were introduced, and in time we were married. Once again I could enjoy country life, and began helping my husband and his father with the family farm. My husband and I have been blessed with two daughters and two granddaughters. Just as I was raised with a strong work ethic, we have tried to instill the importance of family and work in our daughters.

We may not always understand what God has planned for us and why some doors close while others open. Essentially, our job is simply to trust and follow where he leads us.

—Lois Voth

Borscht is best described as cabbage soup with meat. There are many variations of borscht. Some recipes use beef while others call for chicken. Some Mennonite ethnic groups use beets as the main ingredient rather than cabbage. Whichever ingredients are chosen, it is best when eaten with a slice of warm crusty bread. The soup is even better on the second or third day, when the flavors have had an opportunity to blend. The following recipe is one that was used by Lois Voth's family.

# BORSCHT

INGREDIENTS:
2 pounds beef with soup bone
2 quarts water
2 teaspoon salt
1 tablespoon vinegar

DIRECTIONS:
Simmer 2-3 hours. Remove bones from broth and set aside. Set kettle in a cold place to harden the fat. Remove fat. Measure out six cups of broth and return to soup kettle.

Add:
1 large onion, chopped
1 cup tomato sauce or 2 cups stewed tomatoes
1 quart, (1 pound) cabbage, coarsely chopped
5 cups cubed potatoes
2 sprigs parsley

Secure in bag or soup ball:
5 peppercorns
3 sprigs dill (1 tablespoon dried dill weed)
1 bay leaf
1 teaspoon salt
$1/2$ teaspoon pepper
2 teaspoons apple cider vinegar
1 cup sweet or sour cream (optional)

Drop spice bag into soup. Simmer until vegetables are tender. Cut meat from bones and add to soup. Simmer a few minutes longer to blend flavors. Remove spice bag before serving and add salt and pepper if needed. Remove from heat and add cream and vinegar if desired.

I was born in the city of Chania, Crete, just south of Greece in the Mediterranean Sea. The youngest of six, I was named Theodora Damoalakis. Theos meaning "God" and "dora" meaning "gift." So as you can see, I was a gift from God from the beginning.

In 1969, I met my future husband. Larry had come to Greece as a volunteer through MCC and was to help the Greek farmers improve their agricultural methods. He was assigned to work on a farm where my brother-in-law was employed. After some time, we married and lived in Greece for one year.

Because I grew up in a city, coming to Kansas was quite a geographical shock. My initial thought was that I was in a place of exile surrounded by nothing. Where were all the people? It was so quiet! Eventually, I grew to love the beautiful big skies, the rolling wheat fields, the peaceful nature surrounding my home, and a pleasant place to enjoy a garden and gorgeous flowers.

In Kansas, I experienced many firsts. The first morning after I arrived, I was greeted by a winter wonderland of snow. I also learned how to drive Larry's 1967 Ford Mustang, a stick-shift no less. Other firsts included a new way of cooking, unusual foods, and a new language in a very different culture. Slowly, I learned to read English, and eventually I would adopt my own language that my children would refer to as "Greenglish," a combination of Greek and English.

In time, however, I began to miss the sea, my family, and the Greek Orthodox religion. While the Mennonite community was wonderful, my heart needed time in Greece. So we returned to Greece, and then later made the decision to come back to America when our oldest son was ready to begin school.

After our three children were in school, I entered the workforce and worked as a cook for the Goessel school district. I then took a job at Bethesda Home in Goessel and later became the dietary manager.

I have learned that even though Mennonites and Greeks are very different, there are also many similarities. Although I am still getting used to the various styles of worship, church is a big part of both communities, and each teaches the value of faith. The differences? Greeks just do things louder. Restaurants are louder. Churches are louder.  Parties are louder. Not better…just LOUDER!

Although I still miss my homeland and the culture I grew up in, I also realize how blessed I am. My father's teachings, my faith, and religion, family and friends helped me through the difficult and challenging times. Today I'm not that much different from any other American wife, mother, or grandmother. So I guess you might say you can take the woman out of Greece, but you can't take the Greek out of the woman.

—Dora Goerzen

# BAKLAVA

## INGREDIENTS:
2 cups finely chopped walnuts
2 tablespoons sugar
½ teaspoon cinnamon
¾ cup to 1 cup canola or corn oil –
   *Do not use olive oil because it has a heavy smell and changes the flavor.*

1/8 teaspoon cloves
1/8 teaspoon allspice
1 lb. box of fillo

## DIRECTIONS:
In a bowl combine the walnut, sugar and spices. Place a sheet of fillo on a wooden board and brush with oil. Make sure to brush the entire sheet.
Add another fillo on top and brush with oil. Continue this until you have used five fillo sheets. Sprinkle filling thinly over half of the dough. Roll the dough like a jelly roll.

Line a baking sheet with foil. Place the roll cut side down on the baking sheet. Brush with oil and refrigerate for about 15 minutes. With a sharp knife, score the chilled dough into diagonal pieces about 1 inch wide and 1/8 inch down. Be sure not to cut all the way through to the filling before baking the rolls.

Bake at 350° for about 35-45 minutes. Let cool. When completely cooked, pour hot syrup over each roll. Let stand overnight before serving, so the syrup penetrates the rolls.

## INGREDIENTS FOR SYRUP:
2 cups sugar
1 cup water
3 tablespoons honey
1 2-inch stick cinnamon (optional)

2 whole cloves
1 teaspoon lemon juice
2 tablespoons brandy

## DIRECTIONS:
Combine all ingredients except lemon juice and brandy in a small saucepan. Bring to boil and simmer gently 8 minutes. Add lemon to syrup, and simmer for two more minutes. Add the brandy and simmer 1 minute. Let the mixture stand for a minute. Remove spices. Pour over cold rolls.

Faith, family, and heritage have shaped my life. I was fortunate to be raised on a farm and enjoy rural living.

When the weather permitted, we walked or biked to the country school that was one-half mile from where we lived. I had only one classmate but have fond memories of Christmas programs, spelling bees and Young Citizen League meetings and end-of-the year field trips.

My family faithfully attended a Mennonite church. In my spare time I loved to read, and the church library was filled with many books that caught my attention.

I received my high school education at Freeman Academy in Freeman, South Dakota. Music, Bible, and Mennonite history influenced my life during this time as my faith continued to grow. My education continued at Freeman Junior College, and I earned my Elementary Education degree from Sioux Falls College.

Being born into a Swiss Mennonite family, I enjoyed many of the traditions that were passed down from my grandmothers. I remember the heavenly aroma of poppy seed rolls, kucken, and bread all baked in a wood stove, when I visited my paternal grandmother. A standard meal for Sunday dinner included cured ham, fried potatoes, stewed apples, and cooked dried beans. My maternal grandmother was a wonderful seamstress. Widowed at an early age, she continued to live on the farm and raise three daughters. Needing extra income, she began sewing for others.

Eventually, I moved to Kansas and did a year of Voluntary Service in Hutchinson. I also worked as a secretary at the General Conference Mennonite Church office in Newton. It was during this time I met my husband, who is a farmer. Now we live on his home place and have been blessed with a son who farms as well.

After we married, I joined Tabor Mennonite Church. I am thankful for the faith my parents and grandparents instilled in me. God has richly blessed us, and I am so grateful. Thanks be to God.

—Lynne Voth

# POPPY SEED ROLLS

INGREDIENTS FOR SWEET DOUGH: Makes five rolls
Dissolve:
1½ cups water (110-115 degrees)     ½ teaspoon sugar
2 tablespoons yeast
Beat together for 8-10 minutes:
¾ cup dry milk                      ¾ cup shortening (Crisco)
½ cup sugar                         3 eggs
1½ teaspoon salt

Add to above mixture 5 cups flour and yeast mixture. Beat well to make soft dough. Place in a greased bowl. Cover and let rise until double. Punch down.

FILLING: Makes two rolls
1 cup poppy seed, finely ground      1 tablespoon flour
¾ cup cream (half-and-half can be used)   1 egg
¾ cup sugar                          1 teaspoon vanilla

Combine poppy seed, sugar, and flour. Add cream and mix. Add beaten egg to the mixture. Cook on low heat until thick, stirring occasionally. Remove from heat and add vanilla. Cool.

To make poppy seed rolls, take 9-10 oz. of dough and roll into an 8 x 13 oblong pan.  Spread a thin layer of filling on dough. Start at the narrow end and roll up tightly. Roll should end up on the seam. Tuck under ends.

Put in metal ice cube tray. Let rise for 10 minutes or so. Before baking make three slits on the top. Bake at 350 degrees for 15-20 minutes. Brush with butter, cool on rack. Enjoy!

*This recipe is used at Schmeckfest at Freeman Academy, Freeman, South Dakota.*

When I was a little girl, I remember sitting in church with Mom and swinging my legs from the pew. Some of the songs that we sang then are still my favorite songs. When "Trust and Obey" was sung, I was puzzled. Why would "Trusttan" not obey? I grew up attending Tabor Mennonite Church and am still a member.

My grade school years consisted of attending a small one-room school where I learned to read. I read all the books in the school library at least once, and I still enjoy books.

Music has also been important to me. I have played piano, clarinet, and bass clarinet as well as giving piano lessons later in life.

After high school, I married the love of my life. Jerry and I were married for nearly fifty years before his untimely death. Two precious daughters joined our family, and now we have two sons-in-law, five grandsons, and two granddaughters. I love it when our youngest granddaughter comes over to visit while her mother works away from home. During this time we play games, paint pictures, write stories, and have other kinds of fun. It gives me a chance to be a young girl again.

Another important part of my life is nature. As a Master Gardener, gardening is always a challenge. I have an interest in bees, and in the past have had several hives. I enjoy watching them and learning how they care for each other. Learning that bees sting when threatened is helpful.

So much can be learned from meeting people and sharing information. I have met many interesting people while working at a bank and the local credit union. I have also worked as a director at Mennonite Heritage Agricultural Museum in Goessel, Kansas.

I always have my camera handy and enjoy taking pictures of God's creatures and his world. On a cold winter day, I enjoy watching the birds gather at the bird feeder. I also enjoy watching the clouds and am amazed at the beautiful configurations they form. God has created the world filled with a stunning backdrop of colors, complete with remarkable creatures and has asked us to care for it.

—Darlene Schroeder

# ZWIEBACK

Those of us who grew up in traditional Mennonite homes also grew up learning how to make zwieback. Zwieback is best described as a double bun that traditionally was made on Saturday. They were served for Sunday breakfast and then again at Faspa, an afternoon light lunch. If there were any leftovers, they were often toasted in the oven. If toasted properly, they could last indefinitely. When Mennonites began to migrate to America in 1874, zwiebacks were packed in sturdy trunks to provide a quick meal during the long ship trip.

Zwieback recipes abound within the greater Mennonite groups. Some original recipes are made only with butter while others use lard and butter. After the dough is mixed and kneaded, it is allowed to rise. Then they are shaped by pinching off a ball of dough and placing it on a pan. A smaller ball is pinched off and pressed onto the first. If the second bun is not pressed on, it could fall off while the bun rises or when it is baked.

## ZWIEBACK

INGREDIENTS:
2 packages dry yeast
1 cup warm water
3 cups milk, scalded
1/3 cup sugar
5 teaspoons salt
½ cup lard or shortening
½ cup margarine
9-10 cups flour

DIRECTIONS:
Dissolve yeast in warm water. Add cooled milk, sugar, salt and melted shortening. Add half of the flour and beat well. Add the rest of the flour gradually; mix. Let rise until double in size. Punch down and shape by pinching off dough to make 1½-inch balls. Place on a cookie sheet 3 inches apart. Pinch off another ball a little smaller and place on top of the first one. The top will fall off unless punched down in the middle with the index finger. Let rise until light and bake at 400° for about 20 minutes. Makes 6 dozen.

I was born and raised on a farm outside of Hillsboro, Kansas. I was blessed with three brothers but always longed for a sister. When I was eleven, my family's life changed forever when my dad died. For the first time in her life my mom found work outside the home. As a result I began to do more of the cooking, laundry, and cleaning. I had watched my mother cook, but preparing a family meal was not something I had ever done. Eventually, through trial and error, I learned some of my mom's secrets to cooking and became more successful. This proved to be a great foundation for my adult life. Now I enjoy cooking for any occasion as our family of nineteen children and grandchildren gathers to enjoy our favorite foods.

I love fall and have always enjoyed purchasing a few pumpkins each year to use as decorations. Eventually, I wondered about the possibility of growing pumpkins on our farm. At the time, my husband wasn't very excited about the idea. Later, I visited with my daughter-in-law about the likelihood of pursuing this notion. Together we began to discuss how this idea might come to fruition. Eventually, Papa's Pumpkin Patch was created.

Every fall our children and grandchildren come home to help with the pumpkin patch. We open the first of October, and people come from our local community and beyond. Visitors can purchase pre-picked pumpkins and gourds or take a trip out to the fields and pick the perfect pumpkin. We also offer food, some being homemade. Games and activities, including a large slide, provide many hours of entertainment.

We invite school groups to visit the pumpkin patch and enjoy watching and interacting with the children as they discover how pumpkins are grown. Opportunities are available for a homemade snack, and everyone looks forward to the hayrack ride to the different pumpkin patches. Each child goes home with a pumpkin.

Each day I am reminded of how blessed I am with my husband, four children, their spouses and our nine beautiful grandchildren. I still enjoy cooking, but my three loves are; spending time with the grandchildren, working on quilts, and working with Papa's Pumpkin Patch in the fall.

—Sharon Unruh

# NEW YEAR'S COOKIES

New Year's Cookies are a pastry that is fried in deep fat. Traditionally they are made on New Year's Day in celebration of the New Year. There are different ways to make the batter, but most are a spongy yeast batter. After the batter has risen, a spoonful of batter is gently dropped into the fat and fried to golden brown. They are best when eaten warm. The following recipe is used at the annual Threshing Day celebration held the first weekend of August, in Goessel Kansas.

INGREDIENTS:

2 cups milk
2 packages dry yeast
¼ cup warm water
¼ cup melted shortening
1½ teaspoon salt

¼ cup sugar
2 eggs
3 to 3½ cups flour
1 cup floured raisins

DIRECTIONS:

Scald milk and cool to lukewarm. Dissolve yeast in warm water and add to the lukewarm milk. Add shortening, salt and sugar. Beat eggs and add. Gradually sift in flour, beating well. Add floured raisins. Let the dough rise for 30 minutes. Stir and beat a little, let rise again until double. Drop a rounded teaspoonful of dough into hot fat and fry until browned.

Repeatedly we have been amazed at the similarities in Mennonite and Greek food. Mennonites who originated from South Russia brought with them a recipe for verenika, a seasoned cottage cheese filled dumpling. The recipe for verenika is on page 59. A similar food in Greece is called tiropita. It is also a dumpling, but generally filled with a cheese, similar to ricotta. Some recipes use fillo dough or a light dough similar to the dough used in verenika. Tiropita and verenika are formed by cutting a three to four inch circle, placing a mound of filling on one side and pressing the edges together.

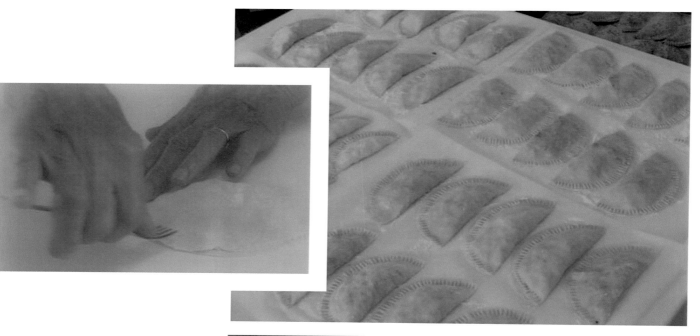

Learning about Greek culture has been part of our journey together. In Greek culture, the preparation of food is significant, but it is the socializing and sharing of the food that is central. Greek meals include a lot of fruits, veggies, bread, and fish. Since red meats are seldom eaten, protein is also obtained from beans and lentils. Traditionally, each town had a neighborhood bakery. Very few homes had large ovens in the kitchen. Many cooks would make dough for as many as nine loaves of bread and let them rise. The younger children then took them to the bakery. Sometimes mishaps occurred, as when a nine-year-old Dora was asked to take the bread to the bakery. On her way, she tripped, fell, and dumped the bread. Luckily, fresh-baked bread was also available for purchase. If any bread was left over at the end of the week, it was fried in

oil and dusted with sugar.

Dora has shared her Greek culture with us in many different ways. One evening she chose to cook a complete meal for us. Together we enjoyed moussakas, a casserole with layers of meat, eggplant and béchamel cream for topping. Béchamel is a thick gravy made with milk, flour, butter and a pinch of nutmeg. It is a typical topping for some Greek casseroles. The meal also included a leaf lettuce salad with Kalamata olives, feta cheese, and Greek dressing. Crusty bread and fruit completed the main meal. Later for dessert, a walnut cake topped with syrup was served. We celebrated in true Greek fashion as we laughed together while sharing a delightful Greek meal.

# MOUSSAKAS

2 pounds of ground beef
1 medium size onion, chopped
½ cup wine (optional)
½ cup parmesan cheese
1 cup bread crumbs
1 14.4 ounce can crushed tomatoes

2-3 eggplant, peeled
3-4 potatoes, peeled
¼ cup fresh parsley, chopped
salt and pepper to taste
béchamel sauce for topping

DIRECTIONS:

Brown ground beef with the onion. Add wine and cook until meat is done. Drain fat. Add tomatoes, parsley, salt and pepper, and let simmer until liquid is absorbed.

Wash, peel and dry eggplants and potatoes. Cut lengthwise into thin slices. Salt and pepper them and then fry with oil until almost done. Remove and set on paper towels.

Lay half of the eggplant and potatoes in neat rows on the bottom of a deep 9 x 13 baking pan. Put half of the bread crumbs and half of the cheese into the ground meat mixture. Then mix and spread over the vegetables.

Lay the rest of the vegetable over the meat and cover everything with the béchamel sauce. Sprinkle with the rest of the cheese and bread crumbs. Pour some drops of melted butter over the top and bake uncovered for about 30-40 minutes at 350° until the top turns golden brown.

# BÉCHAMEL SAUCE

INGREDIENTS:

3 tablespoons butter

4 tablespoons flour

3 cups of milk

salt to taste

dash of nutmeg

DIRECTIONS:

Melt butter over low heat in a small pan. Add flour and mix together with a whisk. Cook while stirring until mixture turns golden brown. Do not burn.

Slowly add warm milk, nutmeg and salt. Whisk until sauce thickens. If sauce has lumps, put in blender to break the lumps.

# GREEK STYLE LETTUCE SALAD

INGREDIENTS:

1 or 2 bunches of leaf lettuce cut into small pieces

3-4 green onions, chopped

Olive oil, enough to coat the vegetables

1-2 teaspoons of wine vinegar

Salt and pepper

Kalamata olives

Feta cheese crumbles

DIRECTIONS:

In a large bowl, mix together cut lettuce, onions, olive oil, vinegar, salt and pepper. Top with olives and feta crumbles.

Put salad together just before serving. It is better when freshly made.

# EASTER BREAD–
# TSOUREKI LAMPROPSOMO

The word Lampropsomo comes from the Greek word, Easter. Lamprn means bright light and psomi means bread. This refers to the light given to us by Christ's resurrection.

Lampropsomo is sweet, egg enriched bread formed of braided strands of dough. Traditionally it is flavored with seeds of Mediterranean wild cherries called makhlepi. Anise seeds can be substituted for the makhlepi.

INGREDIENTS:

1 cup butter
9-10      ½ cups of flour
1          ½ cups of sugar
              1 cup warm milk
                 6 eggs

1 tablespoon finally ground anise seed
    2 packages instant yeast
    1 teaspoon salt
        1 tablespoon grated
            orange and lemon rind

DIRECTIONS:
Dissolve yeast in a small bowl with 1 cup of lukewarm water. Add enough flour to make a thick batter. Cover with a towel and set aside in a warm place and let it rise for about 1 hour.

Place remaining flour in a large bowl and make a hole in the center. Pour the yeast mixture into this hole. Rinse the bowl which contained the batter with warm milk and add it to the flour. Add remaining ingredients, reserving one egg for glazing. Knead for about 10 minutes until smooth. This should make a stiff dough. Add additional flour if necessary. Cover and let rise for about 2-3 hours.

Molding the braids:
Separate the dough into 6 portions about the size of a small orange. Using the palm of your hand, roll each piece on a floured board to a 9" length. Place 3 pieces side by side and braid.

Place in a baking pan and let rise. Brush with a beaten egg and sprinkle with sesame seeds. Bake at 325° for about 35-40 minutes.

*For traditional Lampropsomo a red boiled egg is inserted prior to baking.

*This roadway offers a spectacular view of the Mediterranean Sea when heading to the beach.*

Has anyone ever given you the evil eye? The evil eye is a glance that is believed to have the power that can cause harm to those upon who it falls.

The evil eye occurred in ancient Greece and Rome and can also be found in Jewish, Islamic, Buddhist, Hindu and some Christian cultures. Traditions vary, but children and women are thought to be more vulnerable. Those accused of casting the evil eye are often times blue eyed individuals and old women.

A glass blue eyed charm is available to ward against the evil eye and are still sold in Greece and Turkey. These charms can be pinned to clothing, worn as jewelry, or used as a charm when attached to items that are carried with a person.

The Greek Orthodox Church recognizes the curse of the evil eye and has a special prayer that can be used for those who have fallen under the curse. After a recent visit to Greece, Dora gave us a charm just in case someone gave us the evil eye.

Pattern: The King's Arrival
By: Leanne Anderson of the
Whole Country Caboodle
Quilt Maker: Lois Voth

# OUR HANDS CELEBRATE

*"Let us therefore celebrate the festival, not with the old leaven, the leaven of malice and evil, but with the unleavened bread of sincerity and truth."* —*1 Corinthians 5:8 (ESV)*

Every year at Christmas we look for ways to celebrate. To stop and celebrate is an essential part of any process. It is through celebrating that we can draw closer to those around us.

Everyone is invited to be God's guest at the manger. We are privileged to be a part of God's greatest celebration. Each year God reminds us of his magnificent gift, Jesus.

Christmas is such a sensory celebration. Our hearts are filled with contentment as we hear the sounds of Christmas music and enjoy the laughter of children. The sight of twinkling lights and the warmth of a hug seal our hearts with love. Tables filled with food call our families to gather and thank the Lord for his blessings. It is through this celebration that traditions are established. God expects us to preserve these traditions for future generations.

In some Mennonite homes, it wouldn't be Christmas without the tangy aroma of freshly baked peppernuts. Peppernuts are spicy little holiday cookies about the size of a penny. They might be hard, soft and light, or crisp and crunchy. Original peppernut recipes were accumulated by Mennonite families in Europe. When the Mennonites left the Ukraine for America in 1874, they brought this tradition with them.

Peppernuts are distinctive in that they use a variety of spices. Spices included in favorite recipes could be ginger, anise, nutmeg, mace, cinnamon, cardamom, and clove. Some very old recipes also include black pepper. Traditionally, peppernut dough was mixed shortly after Thanksgiving.

After the dough was mixed, it was packed into five-gallon crocks and stored in the cellar for a week or more. This procedure allowed the spices to blend with the sugar and flour.

Interestingly enough, a cookie made with a variety of spices is also prepared in Greece throughout the Christmas season. Melomakarona, a cookie flavored with orange, lemon, cinnamon, cloves, and honey, fill most houses with a spicy aroma. Sometimes they are also called phoenikia.

Traditionally, most Grecian households did not have ovens, so the cookies were placed on large sheets and taken to the neighborhood bakery. As the aroma of fresh baked cookies filled the streets, neighbors would gather to visit.

Whether eating melomakarona in Greece or peppernuts in the United States, we extend our hands and invite others to share in the celebration of God's greatest gift.

*Christmas*

# CHRISTMAS PEPPERNUTS

INGREDIENTS:

1 cup butter or margarine
4 cups light brown sugar
4 eggs
1 tablespoon soda in 1 tablespoon hot water
7 cups flour

½ teaspoon nutmeg
1 teaspoon cinnamon
¼ teaspoon cloves
3 cups chopped nuts

DIRECTIONS:
1. Cream shortening and sugar until fluffy.
2. Add eggs, one at a time, beating well after each addition.
3. Add water.
4. Sift dry ingredients together.
5. Add half the amount of flour and mix well. Add remaining flour and knead thoroughly. Add nuts.
6. Store dough in tightly covered container in the refrigerator overnight or longer. This helps the dough to season and spices to blend.
7. Roll dough into thin ropes and slice with sharp knife dipped in flour or cold water. Pieces should be about the size of a hazelnut.
8. Place pieces separately on greased baking sheet.
9. Bake at 375° for 7-10 minutes or until golden brown. Baking time depends on how brown you like peppernuts. Different degrees of browning change flavor and texture of peppernuts.

*"Peppernuts were baked early and put in a flour sack. Then they were hung on the ceiling rafters until Christmas. They were not given as gifts because everybody made them."*

*—Member of Tabor Church*

I obtained this recipe from my mother-in-law, Marna Abrahams. The original recipe also had star anise but my family enjoys the subtle, nutty flavor without the anise. —Ilona Abrahams

# CHOCOLATE PEPPERNUTS

INGREDIENTS:

1½ cups sugar
½ cup oleo
2 eggs
4 tablespoon buttermilk
3 cups flour
1 teaspoon soda

2 teaspoon cinnamon
½ teaspoon cloves
3 tablespoons cocoa
1 teaspoon vanilla
1 cup ground raisins
½ cup chopped nuts

DIRECTIONS:

1. Cream sugar and oleo.
2. Add eggs and buttermilk.
3. Sift flour, soda and cocoa together. Add cloves and cinnamon to flour. Add to creamed mixture.
4. Stir in raisins and nuts. Add the vanilla.
5. Make long ropes and chill.
6. Slice long ropes into small pieces and place on cookie sheets.
7. Bake at 375° for 7-8 minutes.

—Darlene Schroeder

*"Usually we rolled them. Four or five were lined up, and all were cut at the same time. If we wanted some that were more uniform, we used a thimble."*

*—Member of Tabor Church*

# HEIN PEPPERNUTS

## INGREDIENTS:

¾ cup shortening
1½ cup brown sugar
1½ cup white sugar
½ cup milk
1 cup chopped walnuts
½ cup chopped gumdrops (optional)

3 eggs
¾ teaspoon cream of tartar
5 cups flour (approximately)
¾ teaspoon baking soda
1 teaspoon vanilla

## DIRECTIONS:

1. Cream shortening and sugars. Add eggs.
2. Beat in flour, cream of tartar, and soda.
3. Add milk and vanilla. Stir until smooth.
4. Stir in nuts (and gumdrops if desired).
5. Roll into long, thin rolls. Chill.
6. Cut into small pieces and place on cookie sheet. Bake in 375° degree oven for about 8 minutes.

—Sharon Unruh

*"Most of our peppernuts were not hard, but I knew some people that made hard peppernuts and then dunked them in coffee."*

*—Member of Tabor Church*

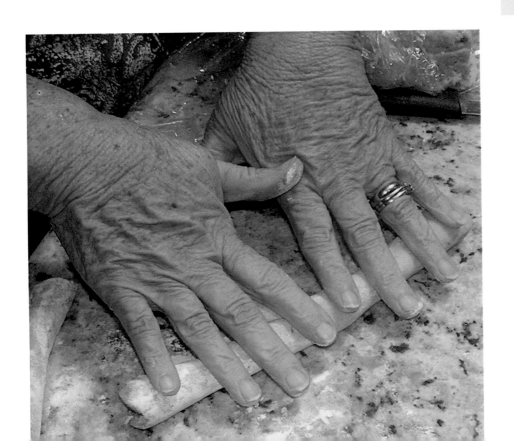

# GRANDMA'S RAISIN PEPPERNUTS

INGREDIENTS:

1 1/2 cups sugar
1/2 cup butter
2 eggs
1 cup raisins, ground
1 teaspoon nutmeg
1 cup coconut, ground
1 cup peanuts or walnuts, ground

1/2 teaspoon baking soda
1 teaspoon baking powder dissolved
  in buttermilk
2 tablespoon buttermilk
2 and 2/3 cups flour

DIRECTIONS:

1. Cream sugar and butter until fluffy.
2.  Add eggs, fruit and nuts. Add the baking soda dissolved in buttermilk.
3. Sift dry ingredients and blend into batter.
4. Chill dough for several hours or overnight.
5. Roll dough into thin ropes and slice with a sharp knife.
6. Bake at 375° for 10 minutes or until golden brown.

A fancy peppernut with raisins, coconut and nuts.

—Lois Voth

*" My mother baked peppernuts in the oven of a four-burner kerosene kitchen stove because we had no electricity or gas."*

*Member of Tabor Church*

# CRISP PEPPERNUTS

INGREDIENTS:

1 cup butter
1½ cups sugar
2 eggs
2 tablespoons syrup
2 teaspoon baking soda
3¾ cups flour

1 teaspoon cinnamon
1 teaspoon ginger
½ teaspoon cloves
½–1 teaspoon oil of anise or ground anise

1. Cream shortening and sugar until fluffy.
2. Add eggs one at a time. Beat well after each.
3. Add other liquids.
4. Sift dry ingredients with spices and flour.
5. Add half the amount of flour, mixing well.
6. Add remaining flour and knead thoroughly.
7. Store dough in tightly covered container in the refrigerator overnight or longer. This helps the dough to season and spices to blend.
8. Roll dough into thin ropes and slice with a sharp knife dipped in flour or cold water. Pieces should be about the size of a hazelnut.
9. Place pieces separately on greased baking sheet.
10. Bake at 375° for 7 minutes.

The light, buttery, crispness and the delicate
flavor of anise makes these peppernuts a Yule time favorite.

— Lynne Voth

*"Mother made them in early December while we were in school. She would make more than one recipe. Oh, they were so good."*

*—Member of Tabor Church*

*Recipe originally published in Peppernuts Plain and Fancy copyright© 1978 by Herald Press, Scottdale, Pennsylvania.*

# MELOMAKARONA

INGREDIENTS:

1 cup Crisco

¾ cup corn oil

1 cup sugar

Grated rinds of 1 orange and 1 lemon

1½ teaspoon baking soda dissolved in ¾ cup orange and ¼ cup lemon juice.

6 cups flour

2½ teaspoons cinnamon

½ teaspoon cloves

FOR THE SYRUP:

1 cup sugar

1 cup honey

2 cups water

1 piece of orange peel

1 piece of lemon peel

1 stick of cinnamon

FOR THE TOPPING:

Mix 2 cups of coarsely ground walnuts with 2 teaspoons of cinnamon, ½ teaspoon ground cloves and 3-4 tablespoons of sugar.

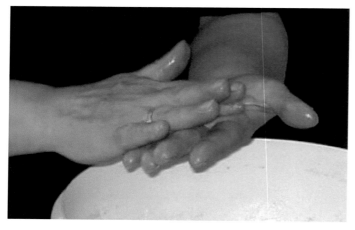

DIRECTIONS: Preheat oven to 350°
In a mixer beat oil, Crisco, and sugar until white and thick. Add orange, lemon juice, and soda mixture. Continue to beat while adding the rest of the ingredients. Turn the mixture onto a floured surface and knead gently.

Take a tablespoon full of dough and shape it into oval cookie about 2½ inches long. Press down with a fork to make horizontal lines. Place them on a cookie sheet and bake for about 15-20 minutes. Place on a rack and let cool.

MAKE THE HONEY SYRUP:

In a saucepan bring sugar, honey, and water to a boil. Add the orange and lemon peel and cinnamon stick. Simmer for 10-15 minutes. Remove from heat.

TO FINISH COOKIE:

Place 2 or 3 cookies in a large slotted spoon and dip them in the syrup. Do not let them soak for too long. They should absorb some syrup yet remain crunchy. Place them on a serving dish and sprinkle with the walnut topping. These should keep for about two weeks.

— Dora Goerzen

# AFTERWORD

Forrest Gump said, "Life is like a box of chocolates. You never know what you're gonna get." And so it is. One day a person is paddling along observing the shimmering stillness of a river, and then the next day struggles to ride out the rapids. Each of those days is a blessing. Our job is to understand why even the bad day is a blessing.

As adults, we've enjoyed each other's company. Laughed with each other, wondering why anyone would choose blue and brown for a quilt top, when orange and green would have to be better. We have admitted that even though we enjoy the combinations of colors, we could never paint a colorful picture. We have realized that someone could thoroughly enjoy quilting all day, sometimes all weekend, while someone else would find enjoyment picking through dirty, dusty, old history books. We acknowledge how cooking for a particular diet can be a challenge while the rest of us enjoy cooking with few restraints. We have come to terms with the fact that even with many hours of practice, most of us will never be able to cook Greek food. At least not authentic, edible, absolutely the best you've ever tasted. And recognize that family businesses, which not only include your family but hundreds of other people, can be life-giving as well as life-draining.

It's easy to see how the creamy, caramel chocolate day is a blessing. But, what about those chocolates you bite into and then look for a place to spit it out. Where is the blessing in those days? The blessing is there, even though sometimes it seems hidden within the decorative wrapper. The blessing is friends. The blessing is sharing those bitter chocolate days with them and knowing they are walking beside you.

# The End